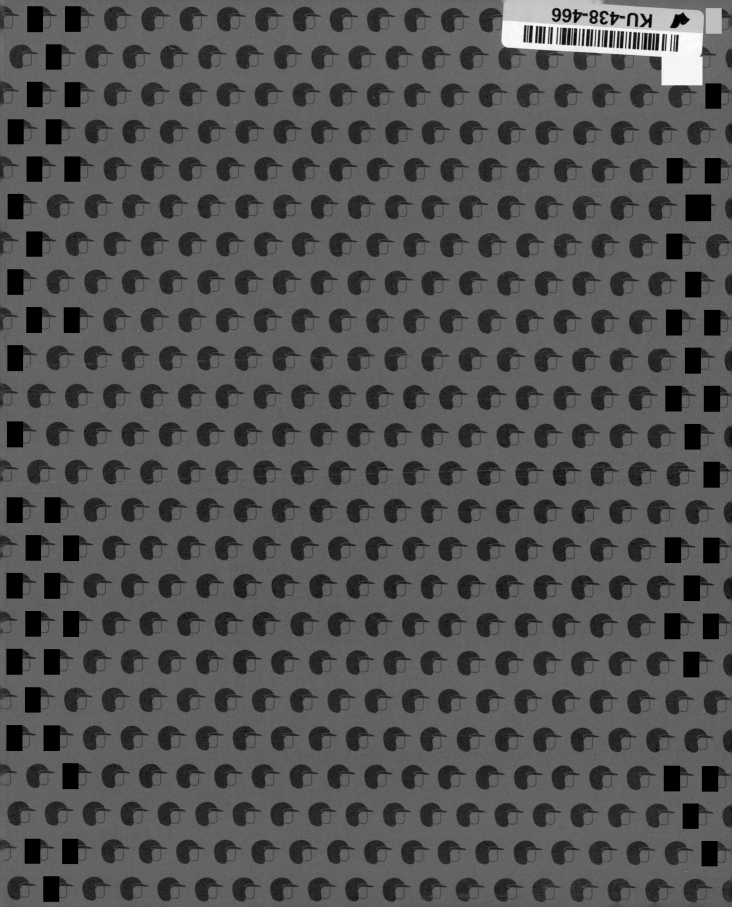

June 4th 1967 — Race-Circuit of Zandvoort
organised in accordance with the stipulations of the International Sporting
Code of the Fédération Internationale de l'Automobile (F.I.A.) and the
supplementairy regulations issued by the KNAC/N.A.V.

ENTRY FORM

X .... TEAM LOTUS LIMITED ....

of (address) ..... NORWICH, NOR 92W, NORFOLK, ENGLAND.

hereby enter the following car for the Grand Prix of the Netherlands 1967.

Make of Car ..... LOTUS .... Make of engine ... Information to

Bore in mm ... Information to .... Stroke in mm .... follow ....
     follow

Cubic capacity in cc .... Number of cylinders ...." ....
                   "

F.I.A.-licenses 1967   Issued by ....

Competitor .... TEAM LOTUS LIMITED .... No. 67/91

Driver .... GRAHAM HILL .... No. 00011

Spare driver .... JIMMY CLARK .... No. 00093

I declare that the above car meets alle requirements of the present „International Formula I", established by the C.S.I.

I hereby undertake to adher to and be bound by the Regulations governing the Race, with which Regulations I declare to be conversant.

I agree that the KNAC/N.A.V. is not responsible for any damage to or loss of the car entered, its parts or accessories, or for any damage that I, my driver, my attendants or my vehicle may cause; and I waive any right of action at law against the KNAC/N.A.V. for any damage I may sustain in consequence of any act or omission on the part of the said clubs or of its officials, representatives or agents, with respect to this competition or to any matter arising therefrom.

I declare that, with regard to the conditions of the race and the nature of the course, the driver(s) is (are) competent in all respects and the car entered is suitable and safe at the speed of which it is capable.

Signature of Competitor :   Signature of Driver :

Stamp of the National   Signature of spare driver, if any :
Automobile Club :

Date,

   28th March   **1967**

NOTE: SIGNED ON THE UNDERSTANDING THAT A MUTUALLY SATISFACTORY MONETARY AGREEMENT IS FINALISED BETWEEN ORGANISERS AND ENTRANT FOR THIS CAR(S) AND DRIVER(S)

JIM CLARK

TRIBUTE TO A CHAMPION

BY

Eric Dymock

First published in Great Britain in 1997 by
DOVE PUBLISHING
Old Chapel House, Sutton Veny, Wiltshire BA12 7AY

First trade edition reprint published by G. T. Foulis & Company, an imprint of
Haynes Publishing, Sparkford, Nr Yeovil, Somerset BA22 7JJ.

Designed by Andrew Barron & Collis Clements Associates

British Library Cataloguing-in-Publication Data. A catalogue
record for this book is available from the British Library.

ISBN 0 85429 982 3

Library of Congress catalog card no. 96-79738

Colour separation by Fotographics Ltd,
London and Hong Kong

Printed in Hong Kong by Midas Printing Limited

Illustrations
Above: Borders landscape.
Opposite: Top right, Jim Clark 1967.
Centre left, from cartoon strip by Boiven Duffar.
Bottom right, Kilmany sculptor David Annand created
life-size bronze statue to be erected at Clark's birthplace.
It was based on a favourite photograph of his mother's,
taken in 1967 the last time he raced at Spa.

CONTENTS

FOREWORD

Ford Motor Company is in motor racing for the stimulation it provides to our technology. Yet there is another less obvious reason. Ford likes to be associated with winners, and there never was a winner in motor racing to match Jim Clark. Eric Dymock's book is a tribute to his great career in which Ford played its part, from the early days on the farm with Ford tractors which the Clark family bought from Jock McBain, the local Ford dealer.

McBain played a crucial role in giving Jim Clark a start in motor racing, which led to him joining Team Lotus and his spectacular performances in the Ford Lotus Cortina. The consummation of the relationship came with the Ford Cosworth DFV engine and its victory in its first race. It was a feat, unmatched in modern grand prix racing, of which Ford remains extremely proud. Jim Clark was at the wheel then and in a sense he is at the wheel now, still providing inspiration at Ford for success 30 years after that great day at Zandvoort.

I went to school in Edinburgh, at Boroughmuir, ironically within a few hundred yards of Merchiston Mews, home of Ecurie Ecosse, the team that scorned Jim Clark in his early years. Growing up in Scotland gave me an insight into the influences that shaped Jim Clark's character and made him not only peerless as a racing driver, but deeply respected by his fellow drivers and adored by his countless fans. His genuine modesty throughout his great exploits at Indianapolis will never be forgotten in America.

This book is a celebration of Jim Clark's life. Ford is delighted to be so closely identified not just with a winner, but a winner with such integrity, such charisma, and such quality.

Sir Alex Trotman
Chairman and Chief Executive Officer, Ford Motor Company

Brooding. Introspective. Jim Clark's engaging shyness concealed deep unease.
A Benno Müller study catches his mood.

AUTHOR'S PREFACE

"**I** was conscious of a profound sense of relief. At last I had the authority to give directions over the whole scene. I felt as if I were walking with destiny, and that all my past life had been but a preparation for this hour and for this trial."

Grand words: Winston Churchill's when he became prime minister in 1940. They convey some of the conviction with which I write about Jim Clark. I may not have been called upon to save the nation, but reinstating the memory of the noblest of racing drivers is a worthy cause. I spent quite a lot of my life preparing for it in a way, from writing about Clark's career when I was a journalist, to writing a book with Jackie Stewart when he won his first world championship.

There is inevitably a strong Scottish thread running through this book. Ford Motor Company's counsellor to both Clark and Stewart, and also Tom Walkinshaw who joined a notable inventory of Scottish drivers that included Ron Flockhart, Archie Scott Brown, Innes Ireland, Ninian Sanderson, and Gerry Birrell, was Walter Hayes: "I have a theory. There was something essentially Scottish in Jimmy. Look at the motor racing talent that has come out of Scotland. There must be a reason for it, even if it is indefinable and elusive."

Heather Rally, 1955. Ian Scott Watson and Jim Clark (DKW) follow Jowett Jupiter. Stuart Parker and Eric Dymock (in white sweater) await turn with Austin Atlantic. Marshal leaning over car is Bill Cleland, father of UK touring car champion John Cleland.

Scotland is a small country. Anybody closely connected with motor racing or rallying in Scotland sooner or later met everybody else, which is how I came to know Jim Clark and Jackie Stewart before either of them ever got into a racing car, and also before I wrote a single word for publication anywhere.

There is another reason for taking a new look at the life and times of Jim Clark. In the 30 years following one of his great race wins, the first victory on its first race of the Ford-Cosworth engine in the Lotus 49 at Zandvoort on June 4, 1967, motor racing changed almost out of all recognition. He would scarcely recognise the be-winged ground-effect cars

that evolved, although some reminders of the old days remain, notably a leading racing engine with FORD on the cam covers. He pioneered a whole dynasty of engines that will ring in the advent of the new millennium and only ring out well into it.

I met Jim Clark in Edinburgh in the spring of 1955, at a briefing of the nascent Ecurie Agricole, a motor sporting team of farmers in the forthcoming Scottish Rally. I was not a member, I was not a farmer or even a journalist; I was co-driving a rival car and it seemed a good idea to evaluate the opposition. The group comprised Neil Brown who raced a black and white TR2, Ian Scott Watson, a founder of Ecurie Agricole, Ronnie Dalglish, a farmer from Auchterarder, and Jim Clark.

Graham Gauld was sports editor of *The Motor World*, Scotland's weekly motoring magazine, and took the group photograph at his parents' house in Edinburgh's elegant George Street. The future champion was fresh from one of Scotland's leading public schools so I concluded perhaps unwisely that his family must be well-off. It was a good time for farmers, and many in the Borders sent their sons to Loretto, with its ochre-washed walls, near Musselburgh, the 11th-century fishing port along the coast towards North Berwick.

It was a breezy group. Robust, smiling Dalglish was a regular and successful rally competitor. Neil Brown, with a girl whose name alas has faded into obscurity, raced with more zeal than fortune. He left Scotland and went to America as a stockbroker but kept up an interest in motor racing and 12 years later went to the American Grand Prix at Watkins Glen. As he walked through the paddock, a hand was clapped to his shoulder. Jim Clark whom he had not seen for years was now one of the greatest drivers of the age. He said, "Hello Neil, what the hell are you doing here?" The gesture said more about Clark than the volumes that have been written about him. It made Neil Brown, like so many of us, an admirer for life. Not a wholly unqualified admirer, but an admirer just the same.

In 1955 Jim Clark was 19, two years younger than I, and he made a deep impression on me largely because he drove his own Sunbeam Mark III. My father, like Jim's a former kirk elder and a slightly stern though mellowing Presbyterian, thought it ill-suited me to have free use of the family Wolseley.

The evening in Edinburgh was scarcely significant as a portent of motor racing history, or even much of an indication of what might transpire in the Scottish Rally. Ian Scott Watson was entered in his DKW, an eccentric choice I felt because like Jim he seemed able to have whatever car

Pre-rally conference, Edinburgh 1955.
Back row from right, Jim Clark, Ian Scott Watson, and Ronnie Dalglish.
Front row from right, Neil Brown, his friend remembered alas only as Maureen, and Eric Dymock.

he wanted. Other members of Ecurie Agricole were either farmers like Oswald Brewis and the Somervail brothers, racing against well-connected members of the motor trade like Ian Skelly, whose family business was to be one of Britain's biggest and most successful Ford dealerships.

I got to know Jim quite well on that Scottish Rally, we were in closely-adjoining cars, but I saw little of him between 1956 and 1958 when I was doing National Service with the Royal Artillery. As a farmer he was spared that inconvenience. By the time I returned he was a rising star. Nobody could guess how far he would go. Graham Gauld said he was marvellous, but then Graham, an arch-enthusiast who played interminable LPs of racing-car sound effects for pleasure, reckoned everybody in motor sport was marvellous.

When I met him next at a sprint near Hawick in June 1958, Jim Clark still had the same cheery nature, revealing nothing of the shock he had endured barely two weeks before, in his first race abroad at Spa in Belgium. One of my schoolboy heroes Archie Scott Brown had died there; I suppose I thought racing drivers took such things in their stride. I suppose I thought we all did.

I never grew as close to Jim as he was to the French journalist and editor of *Sport Auto*, Gérard (Jabby) Crombac, a great friend and staunch admirer. I cast off my engineering job to write about cars, and by the 1960s was covering many of his British races as a staff member on *The Motor* in London. By the 1960s I was grand prix correspondent of *The Guardian*, a grown-up journalist I felt, and it was some time before Jim could make up his mind whether to treat me like the rest of Fleet Street, coldly, or accept me as an old countryman from 1955. I guess among my saving graces was that I continued to write in Scotland for *Top Gear*, the magazine of the Scottish Sporting Car Club – not its 1990s counterpart of the same name.

Often we simply kept clear of one another. It was easier, and I knew that were I to exploit the old connections the relationship would not prosper. I enjoyed a rapport with Graham Hill, Jack Brabham, Bruce McLaren, and other drivers, mechanics, team managers, and hangers-on in the grand prix circus. They got to know my face because I was there, some of them remembered my name or at least that of the newspaper I wrote for. I rather doubt many of them read much that I wrote. Graham Hill did because he liked to know that sort of thing. If Jim Clark did he never mentioned it, which means he did not find anything to complain about. Jabby said he read the British press in the office of *Sport Auto*.

I was careful never to ask Jim anything he would not tell any

Motor racing at Charterhall. Stirling Moss had just become first British driver to win a world championship grand prix.
Winners on 6 August 1955 included
Bob Gerard (Maserati), Desmond Titterington (Jaguar), Reg Parnell (Aston Martin), and Archie Scott Brown (Lister-Bristol).

Jim Clark at Cortina d'Ampezzo
celebrating Cortina successes.

journalist – there was no pulling of old Scottish friends' status – and the ploy seemed to work. Sometimes it would be days before the Fleet Street barrier was breached and we would talk easily. It was a fencing match we went through. I knew the taboo areas, money, danger, his racing secrets, and although he enjoyed sharing racing gossip it was always easier if it was about people and not about technicalities.

By 1965 we had re-established something like the old empathy. Jackie Stewart was a help. I knew his brother Jimmy, gentlemanly Jimmy, before Jackie ever raced, and he reassured Jim Clark that I was unlikely to write the sort of Fleet Street reportage he despised. David Benson who had been deputy editor at *The Motor* and in whom Jim had confidence, was similarly reassuring, and by the end of 1966 it was quite like old times. Jim treasured fellow-Scots almost as much as we treasured him.

Jackie Stewart had arrived in front-rank racing in 1964, declining to join Jim at Lotus after driving in Formula 2 and going instead to BRM for 1965. His friendship with Jim was lifelong and firm although there were some things about him Jackie never understood. Clark and Team Lotus were under contract to Esso, Stewart and BRM were with Shell. Stewart used to lunch in the congenial company of Esso racing manager Geoff Murdoch at his paddock marquee where the food was better than BRM's. He would watch in amazement at Jim consuming steak and chips before a race. Jackie was at a loss to know why he ignored the perils of a heavy meal. A driver could choke on the contents of his stomach in an accident. Stewart consulted doctors and crash experts and in any case believed racing hungry made him faster. How very different they both were.

Stewart felt that Jim set himself up for motor racing in a curious way. He prepared himself very deliberately, as though he was trying to make racing somehow unimportant. He was tense, nervous, uneasy, as his famous nail-biting revealed. "He was constantly doing it," said Stewart. "Nobody ever knew what was going on inside him. He was an incredibly private person, he hardly ever confided in anybody. There were quite a lot of things that you could not discuss with Jim. You didn't talk about money, you didn't talk about dangers of motor racing. He confined things like that to himself so much, that you worried that they were consuming him from inside. He isolated himself. You could see the anxiety in his shoulders. He had a stiffness in his shoulders. He was never what you could call a loose guy and it got worse as he got older."

Clark found it difficult to relax, to be comfortable with people, which was why he never liked public speaking. Stewart by contrast seemed to enjoy performing in front of audiences and was fond of telling about driving with Clark in Australia and coming to an unguarded railway crossing in the desert where the line stretched empty as far as the eye could see in both directions. Jim brought the car to a shuddering halt, looked both ways along the unoccupied track and enquired nervously in a small voice, "What do you think Jackie?"

He constantly asked other people to help him with decisions. "He needed me," said Stewart, "Even when there was nothing coming! He needed people to help him through problems and some of these problems were imaginary. Sometimes there was no crisis. He had nothing to worry about."

Jim did not like to appear competitive. He thought it rude or pushy or aggressive. He was always competitive in a racing car although never aggressive. Other drivers respected him for his speed and accuracy; they tended to give way to him because he was quicker or out-manoeuvred them, they never feared him or felt they had to get out of his way lest he push them off the road. It was an essential feature of Jim Clark's track-craft. Jackie Stewart never saw him, strictly speaking, as naturally competitive strangely enough, much as he did not want to appear to be wound up or tense: "He was an incredibly complex man."

Jim Clark played an influential role in Stewart's career. Stewart's important drives with the Ron Harris Lotus Formula 2 team, and the 1964 Rand Grand Prix in a Formula 1 Lotus were crucial and only achieved with Clark's consent and encouragement. "I was driving the same kind of cars, not just to begin with, not only single seaters, but touring cars and Lotus Elans and sports cars, we had a lot in common. Naïve as I was as an up and coming racing driver, I was not as naïve as Jim Clark. He would drive almost for nothing. He was driving for Ian Walker, I was driving for Chequered Flag and I knew what he was getting paid."

The Rand Grand Prix drive came about when Jim strained his back in a snowball fight on a Ford press engagement at Cortina d'Ampezzo celebrating the competition achievements of the Ford Cortina, and was unable to take part. Stewart was searching for a Formula 1 drive but he knew Lotus was Jim's team and there was not room for both of them in it. Chapman in any case could

Driving down the bobsleigh run was relatively safe. Jim Clark strained back in a snowball fight.

CORTINA SALUTE TO CORTINA CHAMPIONS DECEMBER 2nd.-3rd. 1964

probably not have afforded both. Graham Hill joined Lotus later but Jim did not mind because he knew he was quicker.

Clark's determination not to be deceived by rascally lawyers and accountants led to some personal and, in the long, run family misfortune. He felt so secure at Duns, the Border town where he lived, that it led to mistakes and misjudgements. He turned to people there that he felt he could trust, but they turned out in the end to be more naïve than he was. His home-grown accountant and lawyer were not up to the job. They felt their way into off-shore companies and tax-efficient money management. They embraced the jargon and the way of life, but in reality they had been taught most of what they knew from what Jim had picked up.

He never wanted to be burdened with looking after money. He knew he was earning quite a lot by the standards to which he was accustomed, and all he had to do was get somebody he could trust to run things for him. He had grown up in an environment where trust was everything; you believed what people told you, and unless there was proof to the contrary you had confidence in their decisions.

Carfraemill. East v West bread roll throwing in the 1950s.

I suppose like most people I came under the Clark spell. He did not behave much like a celebrity and I could scarcely believe how boisterous he could be, when he was usually described as quiet shy, and retiring. He threw bread rolls at the Glasgow group, of which I was one, at Carfraemill Hotel after races at Charterhall, the Borders circuit in the 1950s, and threw them again at the opposing BRM team in the Hotel de la Ville at Monza in the 1960s. He was not just pretending not to be famous; he was genuinely self-effacing and he would appear almost ordinary; one of the lads, unassuming. In practical terms he could not be completely anonymous of course. He was followed everywhere by autograph hunters. Sightseers crowded hotel lobbies just to catch sight of him. Men smiled a wan hero-worship sort of smile and made way for him. Girls swooned, especially when he laughed, which was often. His face lit up and his dark eyes flashed and sparkled.

By 1966 he had learned how to cope. He could put people at ease when he cared to, but he found it difficult to be completely unpretentious. He was world champion after all, and whatever doubts he may have entertained by then about not being the best and fastest driver on the planet, he kept strictly to himself. He could certainly be entertaining company and he loved to talk cars; it was only when he was involved with Colin Chapman, Lotus's founder, that I ever saw him tense. If Chapman beckoned in the racing team's paddock, Jim complied, not subserviently, but because the pair were in a firm partnership, a symbiotic relationship in which each was completely dependent on the other.

Having people round him that he knew eased the stress that motor racing brought Jim Clark. Away from home, it was sometimes perceived as indecisiveness, although his sister Betty did not find him indecisive: "Don't believe all the stories of his indecision. You could see him make decisions on the farm and he was quick, confident, and knew what he was doing. There was no indecision there."

He was not indecisive when it came to money. Peter Hetherington who handled Jim's financial affairs from 1965 refuted the notion that he was indecisive. "I've heard that said. From my point of view the answer's no, because once we'd made a decision, he never wavered, he said get on and do it."

Barrie Gill, motoring correspondent of the *Daily Herald*, thought of him as the racer's racer, whose obsession with leading grands prix from the start put him at the pinnacle of sport: "Jimmy seemed to go berserk when the flag went down," he said. "Some critics described his race tactics as lunacy, but the flag fall seemed to send the adrenalin leaping and switch on all the physical and mental faculties at peak revs." Gill loved Clark's sporting banter when he was ghost-writing Graham Hill's newspaper column at Deal's Hotel in advance of the South African Grand Prix at Christmas 1962.

The South African race would decide the world championship between Clark and Hill, and Jimmy would keep eyeing Gill's typewriter, "just to see what Graham is going to write about me". There was no bitterness in rivalry, no edge like there was between racing contenders of a later era. Graham Hill offered Clark a drowning contest to settle the 1962 championship, by seeing which of them could remain under water longer in the hotel pool. Clark, a hopeless swimmer agreed provided Hill went first.

When Hill won Clark had to make the loser's speech. He said, "We all knew BRM had to win something this year to remain in business, and we all really wanted them to, but this is ridiculous…" Gill, like most of the racing journalists, even those who occasionally got a studied silence for mis-reporting, hero-worshipped Clark.

These were different views of him among people who were close to him. The diverse ways he touched different people were an essential part of

Graham Hill. "Made a better world champion than
I would have in 1962" – Jim Clark

the enigma of the man. Those who knew him only as a world championship racing driver describe a different Jim Clark from the one at home. "Jim never changed. He was aye the same Jim Clark," was the earnest belief from the homesteaders who rarely saw the dashing international jet-setter.

Jimmy really assimilated quite quickly into this big and exotic world around which there was a huge amount of glamour. There were girls, he was courted by the rich and famous, and even the most retiring and backward country boy could scarcely have failed to enjoy it. There was not only the jet-setting international airline travel and company aircraft, but in due course he mixed with a lot of people who flew their own. Jim learned to fly and had one too. From his background in farming in the 1950s nobody would have been able to see such glories of the outside world. He may not have been much altered by them or influenced by them, but he could not have been unmoved or unaffected. What was certain was that when he met something out there he did not understand, he liked to go back to Duns to think it out.

Patrick Mennem, who edited Clark's writing for the *Daily Mirror* received a call from Jimmy when he was passing through Heathrow. "He asked me to come along for a drink. He'd had a few noggins himself. He would occasionally, although it was rare. But I couldn't persuade him that I couldn't get through to his side of the airport lounge."

To Mennem he seemed highly strung. A Border farmer recast in the beguiling world of motor racing, but still a farmer at heart. He once accompanied Clark to a local market where everybody was a farmer. He had won two world championships, yet nobody mentioned them. All they talked about was sheep. He told Mennem that was what he wanted to go back to. He led others to believe he would not. It was all part of the mystery of Jim Clark. Was he decisive or indecisive? Was he worldly or naïve? He was a genius at the wheel beyond doubt, but was he astute enough to be allowed out into the great cruel world of motor racing, where a person's word was sometimes only an expression of good intentions?

My father had a stock reply to my reassurances about bringing the Wolseley back on time. "The road to Hell," he would say, "Is paved with good intentions."

Champion magazine hailed Clark as the new Fangio.

Dan Gurney. The only driver whose skill Clark thought matched his own.
The one driver who admired him most.

PROLOGUE AND EPILOGUE

Sunday April 7, 1968, was a grey day in West Germany and in Britain. The Deutschland Trophy race for Formula 2 cars was taking place at Hockenheim, a dull little track carved through thick pine forest with two short straights joined by a long curve, and a complex of hairpins through a stadium. Its most cherished moment came soon after it was opened in 1939, when Mercedes-Benz tried out their 1½litre W 165 cars in secret, before despatching them to triumph in Tripoli.

At Brands Hatch in Kent, the British Racing and Sports Car Club (BRSCC) had persuaded the British Overseas Airways Corporation to put up money for the BOAC 500, a six hour race for sports cars in which the main interest lay in the new Alan Mann Ford V-8 F3L, resplendent in red and gold, competing against Porsches, older Ford GT40s, Lola-Chevrolets and Ferraris, and a solitary screaming gas turbine Howmet.

Derek Bell. New driver with Ferrari. Career crisis.

At Hockenheim it was raining, and so cold that belt-drives for the troublesome fuel metering units kept breaking on the Lotus Ford-Cosworths. Derek Bell, a driver new to Formula 2, was driving a Brabham and finding the conditions difficult. It was the first time the dashing fair-haired Bell, an up-and-coming works appointee for Ferrari, had met Jim Clark who was also staying at the Hotel Luxor in Speyer. Bell sat down to tea after Saturday practice with Jim and Graham Hill, "…me wet behind the ears sitting there with two of my greatest heroes. Jimmy told me, 'Don't get too close when you come up to lap me because my engine is spitting and banging.' I thought, 'This is my idol saying *when you come up to lap me*. It was difficult to take in." Bell was on Dunlop tyres which were superior to the bothersome Firestones on the Lotuses that weekend. He had breakfast with Graham and Jim, and drove with them to the track and that was the last he saw of the man whose example he followed and whose reputation was beyond equal. Bell remembered the Lotus mechanics driving up and down the paddock all morning trying to cure Clark's car's misfiring, and remained convinced that was what caused his accident.

"I think Jimmy was having a terrible time. Running alone, battling with a poor car on tyres which were not working terribly well. I reckon the engine suddenly cut out. He would have automatically applied a touch of opposite lock as the car began to slide – and then the power came back on, the rear end gripped, and the car speared off into the trees."

Clark did not much like Hockenheim. He had said to Graham Hill over dinner: "Anyone who goes off into the trees hasn't got a chance … " He qualified seventh, behind the blue French Matra MS7s of Jean-Pierre Beltoise and Henri Pescarolo who won on the aggregate of the two heats. The track was still damp for the first.

Ford had wanted Clark to drive one of the new Prototypes, the recently-completed F3L in the BOAC 500. Stocky Walter Hayes, pipe-smoking, reflective, clever, a former Sunday newspaper editor who joined Ford as director of public affairs encouraged the company to take part in motor racing and in doing so fostered Jim Clark's career: "The F3L was to have its debut at Brands, and Jimmy was going to drive it. It was all perfectly clear. Then he rang me up and said 'I can't do it. I know I promised you, but Colin says I've got to go to Hockenheim.' And I said, 'Jimmy, Hockenheim is a Formula 2 race, what are you doing in Formula 2?' 'Well, Colin said he'd promised the sponsors.' He would ring me up sometimes when he wouldn't talk to Colin Chapman. He sort of hoped that things would work out."

Two Mann Ford cars were entered, one started. There were muddles over drivers. Jack Brabham could not come because he had a fuel contract with Esso and he sent Jochen Rindt instead. Graham Hill and Jim Clark were contracted to Firestone, and the Mann car ran on Goodyears. It was to have been driven by Goodyear drivers Bruce McLaren and Denny Hulme. In the event it was driven by McLaren and Mike Spence, starting from the front of the grid between two Porsche 907s.

Clark and fans, Barcelona, April 1968.

Dave (Beaky) Sims was Clark's mechanic at Hockenheim, and related what a bleak weekend it had been from the start. Besides the problems with the fuel metering unit drive belts, it had been difficult to get the gear ratios right.

It was the second European Formula 2 race of the season. At Barcelona the week before, Sims and his colleague Mike Gregory had been in charge of Clark's and Graham Hill's cars. Jim qualified his Lotus 48 second fastest, only 0.1sec behind Jackie Stewart's Matra, but he was rammed from behind on the first lap by Jacky Ickx. Clark retired extremely cross, with damaged rear suspension.

Sims: "Was he ever angry! Ickx got his mechanics to put in new brake pads on the grid, and they weren't bedded in. The Ferrari went straight into the back of Jimmy's car at the first hairpin. Graham blew an engine, so we headed for Hockenheim, Mike put a new engine in Graham's car, and I put a new rear end on Jimmy's."

Astute, deliberate, calm. Walter Hayes steered Ford and Clark into conjunction.

In the first heat Clark was in difficulties, and after four laps lay eighth, waving Chris Lambert past in his Brabham. Lambert, soon to die in a crash with Clay Regazzoni at Zandvoort said that when he overtook he thought there was a problem with Clark's engine. On the long curving run to the outer reaches of the track on lap five, Clark accelerated to about 160mph. The only witness was a German official who described how he fought for control before the Lotus plunged sideways off the road into the trees. The impact wrenched the subframe containing the engine and gearbox off the main part of the car.

A course marshal came to the Lotus pit in a Porsche and its driver said to Sims: "Come with me."

"I told him I couldn't, that Jimmy was missing, and he said, 'Yes, I know. Come with me'." The Porsche took him round to the accident, just beyond where the second chicane was later built. The race was still going on. "We got there and I started looking for the car. He pointed into the woods. There was just the monocoque tub lying there. I was only 25, and it was horrific. Like a bad dream. I said: 'Who's taken the engine and gearbox off? Where are they? And then I saw them, yards away. I kept saying 'Where's the driver? Where's Jim Clark?' And that was when the guy said, 'I'm sorry to tell you, but he's dead.' I couldn't believe it."

"Nobody knew what to do. I radioed back to the pits to tell them to bring Graham in, and then he took over. It was Graham who called Chapman who was away skiing. He dealt with all that awful stuff …"

Walter Hayes was given the news as the cars lined up at Brands Hatch. "It was one of the very bad moments of my life, standing in the pits at Brands just as the BOAC 500 was going to start and hearing that Jimmy had died." Hayes had persuaded Ford Motor Company to create the Ford-Cosworth DFV engine and among its express purposes besides giving Ford a new exciting image was to win the world championship again for Jim Clark, and now he was dead of a broken neck.

Motor racing almost died of a broken heart.

The BOAC 500 was a cheerless affair. As the news filtered in from Hockenheim that spring afternoon, a generation slowly began to realise that motor racing would never be the same again. It was more than the death of a driver, it was the end of an era. It was more than a squall that followed a storm. When Jim Clark died the whole climate of motor racing changed.

When the news came through to the Brands Hatch press box, a sensation of incredulity, of incalculable grief, descended like a pall. People who had never met Jim Clark felt a profound sense of loss. Those who knew him were stunned into disbelief. The car he died in was one of the first to bear the livery of a sponsor instead of the traditional British racing green. Gold Leaf Team Lotus marked the arrival of a new force in motor racing, – big money. The fatal crash that reached the front pages of the world's newspapers showed the contrary side. Sponsors wanted to be associated with winning, not with the sudden death of a hero.

As for the unfortunate F3L Alan Mann sports car, it did well in the BOAC 500, taking the lead for most of the first two hours although it gave Bruce McLaren a rough ride on the uneven Brands Hatch surface. When Spence took over it broke a half-shaft and retired. It reappeared at the Nürburgring but crashed heavily injuring Chris Irwin. "It was the only car I ever hated in my life, and the single big mistake I made in motor racing," said Hayes. "Alan Mann said he could do it and it would be cheap and we thought that we needed to replace the GT40 which had been showing its years. We thought we needed to do it although on reflection we didn't need to do anything in sports cars. They were in decline anyway. The GT40 years had been special, like a sort of military campaign. I killed that car out of sheer hatred."

Jacky Ickx and Brian Redman won narrowly in an out-dated Ford GT40.

Theories concerning Clark's accident ranged from freak gusts of wind to errant pedestrians and Bell's hypothesis about the misfiring engine, but the most likely explanation was the explosive decompression of a tyre, throwing the car off course, and sideways into the fatal tree.

Investigations showed that a tyre had lost pressure through a slow puncture, and although centrifugal force kept it in shape at speed in a straight line, side force in the gentle curve caused the beading to loosen from the rim, and drop into the well. Clark was expecting difficulties on the slippery surface, but even he could not keep control. There was no

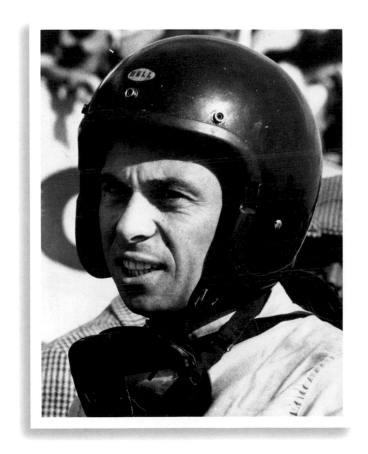

Open face, open helmet.
Jim Clark earned respect and affection on and off the track.

Helen Stewart, Clark confidante.
Jackie Stewart, Clark heir.

safety barrier. Bob Martin racing manager of Firestone and Peter Jowitt of the Royal Aircraft Establishment (RAE) accident investigation branch examined every shred of evidence and came to the same conclusion.

When Clark was killed, the sport cried real tears. At the funeral Jim's father told his great friend and rival, the smiling tall American Dan Gurney, that he had been the only driver Jimmy truly feared. Gurney never forgot it, but typically kept it to himself.

"It destroyed me, really, in terms of my self control," said Gurney. "I was drowned in tears. To hear that from someone whose son had been killed and wasn't there any longer was more than I could cope with. For a long time I didn't say anything about it because I felt it was a private thing and I didn't want to utilise it to sort of glorify my driving ability or reputation, but it was certainly the biggest compliment I ever received."

Jim Clark's long-time girlfriend, already married to Dutchman Ed Swart, heard it on the car radio at Zandvoort in Holland. It was the lead item on the news. "I thought how come they're mentioning a little Formula 2 race and Jim Clark. My Dutch wasn't very good but I knew he'd been injured, and it didn't yet say he was dead. I wasn't sure, and I rushed over to my father-in-law and asked what it meant. He went kind of white and had to tell me. I think by then I knew anyway."

A disc jockey on a radio station in far-away Los Angeles said: "If you are mourning the death of the great driver Jim Clark, put on your headlights". The whole freeway lit up at midday.

Derek Bell won the world endurance championship in 1985, the world sports car championship in 1986 and the 24 Hour classic at Le Mans five times. Tough, craggy, one of the most experienced and determined drivers, he was deeply affected by Clark's death at such a critical stage of his career.

"It made me wonder if I was cut out to be a racing driver. I could not shrug it off. I now know that no driver can shrug it off. They just keep their feelings private." He recalled an occasion at Le Mans after a fatal accident when another seasoned campaigner abruptly said to him, "I sometimes wonder why we do this. Is it worth dying for?"

It was an unwritten rule for drivers never to talk about death at the track. In private perhaps, but not when they were racing. "If I was with

somebody I knew extremely well, like David Hobbs, and we were away from the circuit having a quiet coffee together, it might be something we would touch on. But not at a track."

Bell, like so many of his contemporaries had found it reassuring to know that Jim Clark had survived in motor racing for so long. When his family pointed out the dangers Bell could always say, "Look at Jimmy Clark. Never broke his skin in a racing car accident." When he died everything changed. "Jimmy Clark always got away with it. A driver simply *has* to believe he is going to get away with it. So when it happened to Jimmy it smashed my beliefs and my philosophy."

Like the death of Kennedy, everybody in motor racing remembered what they were doing when they heard about Jim Clark. Jackie and Helen Stewart were moving to their new house in Switzerland overlooking Lake Geneva. Helen, pretty, a little gauche perhaps, fresh, schoolgirlish, not quite the blushing bride but only six years married: "Jackie was in Spain testing and he called me and he said 'Hi, it's me'. He couldn't speak. He put the phone down. There were no words. He just couldn't speak." In 1995 when I talked to Helen, elegant, wiser now, and a close witness to many motor racing tragedies since, the memory was still etched on her mind as clearly as yesterday.

She was not the only person I talked to who was still moved to tears by the dreadful loss on Sunday, April 7, 1968.

Stirling Moss, greatest driver who never won world championship
contemplates Graham Hill who won twice.

VOCATION TO RACE

Born in 1936 Jim Clark became champion driver of the world in 1963 and 1965, and narrowly missed winning twice, perhaps thrice, more through mechanical perversity. He was the first non-American to win the Indianapolis 500 for nearly 50 years, and was the most talented driver of his generation. He was one of a handful in the history of motor racing who could claim to be the best ever, yet one of the few likely ever to do anything of the sort, allowing plaudits to wash over him with an air of embarrassed modesty that never looked contrived.

The ingredients of the Jim Clark personal legend are a catalogue of virtue. He was admired and respected as upright, honest, and sporting, a straightforward Border farmer who campaigned fairly, was magnanimous in victory, modest, shy, retiring, and suffered the occasional defeat serenely. He was a notorious nail-biter and famously indecisive. He could not make up his mind about marrying his long-serving girlfriend Sally Stokes, so she went off and married Ed Swart in 1967 at the motor racing wedding of the year with Graham Hill's and Colin Chapman's daughters as bridesmaids. Damon Hill was a very young guest.

Jabby Crombac understood Clark.

Saintly Ed. He did not want Jimmy to get killed and remain for ever Sally's second option. He would rather have given her up. Ed was a distinguished driver as well as race director for the Dutch Grand Prix, a post that demanded all his proficiency in French, Italian, English, German, and Spanish as well as Dutch. He never flinched from his admiration for his fellow-racer and never stopped racing.

Sally had her own explanation for Clark's indecision. She said he became a different person when he stepped into a racing car, and different again when he stepped out. He was so heavily loaded with natural talent that on the track he took life-and-death decisions instantly. She often asked him in exasperation how he could make up his mind to turn the first corner, and he would reply, "No problem. It comes naturally. It's easy."

"But every time he stepped out of a racing car he left half of himself in it," said Sally. Dichotomy haunted his life. Jabby Crombac summed him

up: "A strange personality. Not altogether what people thought he was like. Everybody imagined him the perpetual nice guy, but he could be a complete bastard if you stepped upon his toes. He could really be a fierce animal."

Friends and admirers freely applied the term 'genius' to his driving. Rivals took Clark's lap times as the benchmark by which to judge theirs. His total of 25 grand prix victories remained a record until 1973 when three-times champion Jackie Stewart exceeded it by a respectful one. Clark's rate of scoring was bettered only by Juan Manuel Fangio and Alberto Ascari.

By any yardstick of motor racing, Clark was one of the greatest drivers in its history. Fangio alone secured a higher proportion of pole positions on his starting grids, and was only narrowly ahead on fastest-lap scoring. Clark's record of seven wins in a season, set in 1963, was not matched until 1984. No driver before or since showed such overwhelming superiority at individual races. Jim Clark gained motor racing's rare 'treble'; starting from pole position, setting fastest lap, and then winning 11 times. This unique achievement started at the British Grand Prix in 1962 and ended at the South African, his final victory in 1968. Jim Clark and the late Ayrton Senna tied for the fastest rate of world championship points-scoring.

Alain Prost took the record of grand prix wins with a total of 51 in an era when there were 16 world championship grands prix in a season. Jim Clark raced when there were around eight championship races and half a dozen non-championship ones run under Formula 1, winning 49 of them. Include his two American Indycar victories and his total of major wins matches Prost's.

Comparisons with drivers of different eras are seldom relevant. Grand prix motor racing passed through many phases. When the great Italian and German drivers Nuvolari and Caracciola raced before the war nationalism was rampant, and team-winning more important than driver-winning. Fangio in the 1950s was a professional, driving in professional teams, often against amateurs. Senna drove in the superheated grand prix hothouse of the 1990s with more races, narrower margins, and huge sums in sponsorship at stake.

Between the times of Fangio and Senna, Jim Clark's period in Formula 1 during the 1960s spanned the change from a few works-sponsored cars racing against a large field of private owners, to a competition between professionally-designed and well-presented works teams mostly outpacing a handful of privateers. Yet by any standard his achievement in winning almost one grand prix in three from 1960 to 1968, starting from pole position 33 times and achieving fastest lap 28 times was astonishing. He came second only once, gaining the remainder of his 274 world championship points by finishing 14 times in the first six.

So as a rule, if Clark's car finished in the points, it finished first. Unlike some drivers, even great ones such as Stirling Moss, he never drove for a non-works team and never appeared at a grand prix in anything less than a well-prepared Lotus. When Team Lotus was waiting for the latest engine from Coventry-Climax or Ford-Cosworth, his cars might have had less chance of winning. One one such occasion he even nursed the heavy H-16 BRM engine to its sole victory, but he never endured whole seasons with under-funded or badly engineered cars.

Accordingly it might be argued that Colin Chapman, dapper David Niven lookalike, the gifted engineer responsible for Lotus cars, was indispensable in determining Jim Clark's success. The two men certainly formed a strong rapport, one a brilliant driver, the other a dazzlingly innovative engineer. They understood one another and worked closely. What Clark would have achieved without Chapman and Team Lotus we shall never know. He may not even have remained in grand prix racing; perhaps he would have chosen a less demanding role, racing purely for pleasure. Perhaps it was the lure of competitive cars that kept him in the driving seat at all, especially during the 1960s when the rate of injury and death among drivers was cruelly severe.

Inspired Clark gave ponderous H-16 BRM engine its solitary grand prix victory.

Notwithstanding the role of Lotus and Chapman in determining Jim Clark's success, his prodigious skill and talent ensured the deep respect of his challengers and the admiration of countless fans.

Dave Sims said: "I hardly ever saw him get mad. He could get uptight with Chapman, and say, 'Look, you should have done this'. He was such a gentleman, and even when things were bad he did not get into a flap, so nobody else did. That way we could get the job done. He was so approachable; out of his driving suit you'd never think he was connected with racing."

It could be frustrating to be in the same team as Clark. One team-mate recalled testing sessions in which he laboriously shaved fractions of seconds off lap times, getting out of the car hot, sweaty, and scared after

Golden moment. Sun glints on the helmets of Jim Clark (left) and Mike Spence.
Faces light up at a quip from Graham Hill. Silverstone, 1967

setting a seemingly unbeatable all-time outright circuit record. Jim would then calmly knock a full second off, apparently without effort. Colleague would put his heart and soul into matching it, drive to his limit and beyond only to find Jim could easily deduct another second. There seemed to be no limit to his resources.

Like Olivier on stage, Clark was so awash with talent that his rivals regarded him as utterly matchless and could aspire only to compete among the also-rans. Team colleague, rival, and fellow-racer Graham Hill was sanguine about Clark's tactics in the opening laps of a race: "What he did was build up an enormous lead and simply try and sap your will to win by making it seem impossible."

He achieved apparent miracles with such ease and in evident safety that when he died the motor racing establishment was deeply unnerved. When he heard the news, Mike Spence, a notable driver in BRMs and Lotuses, echoing Derek Bell, said: "If it can happen to Jimmy what hope is there for the rest of us?" A month later Spence, too, was dead, crushed by the flailing front wheel of his car in a crash at Indianapolis.

In a perceptive comment within a few weeks of the accident at Hockenheim, Graham Gauld, author of books about Jim Clark and a long-standing friend, wrote: "Though to the end he was still a kindly person to those whom he allowed into his confidence, he occasionally displayed a petulance and spite which was generally uncharacteristic. To some people he was cruel, but amidst this cruelty one felt that Clark was trying to punish himself for being unable to explain himself. If he had an unfulfilled wish, it was to be understood by everyone, but to ask that was to ask for the impossible. Though on the face of it he appeared a simple person he was in fact quite a complicated man."

Ian Scott Watson was a fellow Borderer, small, wiry, quick-witted, who set Jim Clark on the road to motor racing fame. He supplied the first cars and organised entries to races, managing Clark's affairs for as long as Jim remained apprehensive about dealing with people he did not know. He did not like the press much. Scott Watson told me: "He was happy with those he knew like yourself and Graham Gauld, but not at all happy with the tabloid press and those who wrote what he regarded as silly articles. The exceptions were David Benson of the *Daily Express* and Patrick Mennem of the *Daily Mirror*. He seemed to hit it off with them."

Jim Clark undoubtedly had something that could be described as genius, even though it is difficult to pin down what it was. It could have been some genetic chemistry, or an unusually well-developed sense of balance. It might have been a special mental perception of speed and distance, a psychological capacity for dealing with stress, or a unique combination of them all. It was not merely quick reactions; plenty of people have these and, with sufficient eagerness or motivation, could be passable racing drivers if they wanted.

Rob Walker employed some of the greatest including Stirling Moss in his long and successful career as a private entrant, and believed the deciding factor for top-class racers was visual acuity. He was convinced that some, like Bernd Rosemeyer, the great German driver of the 1930s, were able to see better than others even in fog. A keen sense of balance seemed to be crucial, and good physical trim a help. Jackie Stewart identified a

Three world champions. Graham Hill, Jim Clark, and Damon Hill (pushing). Henry Taylor and Louis Stanley look on.

faculty for slowing down action, like the frames of a slow-motion film, but he proved able to see better than anybody else in the 1968 German Grand Prix. The treacherous Nürburgring had its Eifel-mountain head in the clouds, the cars were shrouded by impenetrable mists of spray, rain and swirling fog swept the track, yet he finished fully four *minutes* ahead of anybody else.

David Benson, who covered most of Clark's career, testified to the driver's extraordinary eyesight when he wore a tie with a tiny logo, and at 40 feet across a table Clark spotted that he too belonged to the spoof North Bucks Duck Racing Club. "It was a long way to identify a badge no bigger than a fingernail," said Benson.

Keen eyesight was a family trait. Jim's sister Betty with the same dark Mediterranean eyes could keep up with her brother at most sports.

The ingredients that made Moss or Clark so much better than their contemporaries included concentration. The eyes sent messages to the brain with crystal clarity, enabling specially gifted drivers to race and appear relaxed. Stirling Moss would line the car up for a corner 100 yards ahead, then he reckoned his job for that corner was done and he'd look in the grandstands for a pretty girl. Ayrton Senna said that when he was going into a corner, he was no longer thinking of that corner, he was thinking of the next one in the sort of analysis that set great drivers apart.

Yet any credible explanation for a top driver's proficiency must include an exquisite three-dimensional spatial perception enabling them to corner, pitch, and sway in cars, yet maintain their equilibrium. They seemed to have a system of gyros like the instruments in aircraft, so that they still knew which way was up when the world was spinning round them. Don Frey, of Ford Motor Company, who worked closely with Clark at Indianapolis, called him the epitome of a racing driver. "His greatest asset," said Frey, "was his imperturbability. When he was five or 10 years old, a gyro began spinning somewhere inside him and he became his own standard-maker. He was inner-directed. He lived in a world of his own."

An example of Jim Clark's almost miraculous skill was recounted by Maurice Phillippe, the Lotus designer responsible for the 1966 Indianapolis car. During shakedown tests at Snetterton, the windswept airfield circuit in Norfolk not far from the Lotus headquarters at Hethel, Jim spun the car in the fast left-handed corner after the hairpin. Phillippe and Colin Chapman were alarmed, certain that an accident there would damage both the driver and car.

They followed the figure-of-eight tyre marks, but when they reached the spot they could see no sign of debris or driver. The track was bounded by a metre-high earth bank, and they found the car had gone through a gap about 20 feet wide – just enough to let it pass through sideways. It lay on the other side completely undamaged with Jimmy standing beside it looking sheepish and embarrassed.

He admitted a mistake. His Firestone tyres were not warm enough to give their best. Phillippe was intrigued to discover that the black tyre marks turned to grey in the middle of the spin, where he had released the brakes at a critical point in order to put the car through the opening. Jim calmly agreed that he had done it to save the car and himself, and even though Phillippe felt sceptical that any human being was capable of retrieving the situation in such a violent gyration, the evidence was clear before him.

Later in the day when the routine of testing was again under way, the same happened again. Jim spun on the approach to the same corner. The distinctive noise of the big methanol-fuelled V-8 abruptly ceased and the Lotus crew raced across to the scene of what this time must be a disaster, only to find Jim with the same embarrassed expression. Another set of tyre marks betrayed a spin like the first, and once again the undamaged car was neatly parked. The gap in the bank required the utmost precision to avoid contact, yet Jim Clark had managed it twice in the same afternoon. On the first occasion Phillippe was tempted to say, "Jolly good luck, well done." and fix the car. On the second: "I realised then beyond doubt that we had somebody special in the cockpit."

Psychologists defined drivers' motivation to race as a powerful desire

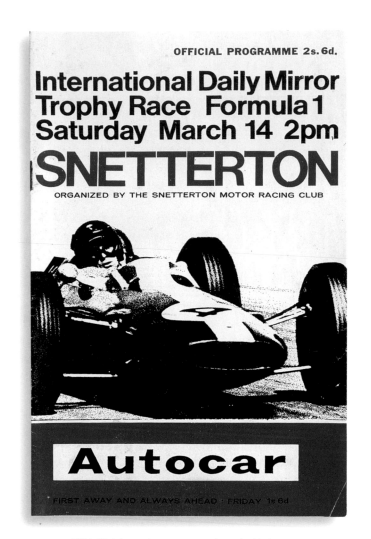

1964. Clark featured on programme but retired in the race.
Won class in a Lotus-Cortina

to have control not just of their cars but, symbolically of their whole lives. In a 1960s analysis of professional racing drivers, the *British Journal of Psychiatry* considered why they did it. Most showed an interest in cars from childhood, like many boys, but, "None (of those interviewed) had had an ambition to be a racing driver as a child. If one considers what is involved in driving, control is an important aspect and this seems to be a considerable personality need in racing drivers. The need to feel in control is satisfied by handling a machine delicately and skilfully at high speeds. Driving at these speeds and performing a task which is obviously dangerous gives rise to a particular exhilaration and a feeling of successful control of objects and oneself."

Unsurprisingly racing drivers were found to be highly competitive, as anybody who saw Jackie Stewart clay-pigeon shooting, or any of them playing table tennis or golf would affirm. "They constantly have to test themselves out against both an internal and external criterion. They compete with each other and each with himself. Even if a driver has lost a race and is lying well behind, he will try to do each lap as perfectly as he and his machine are capable. Almost each week of their lives they take considerable risks of death. They obviously do not consciously think of this, but it seems that it is not enough to compete with other people or against their own inner criterion of perfection. They almost gamble with death, going to the limit, and again this seems to prove that ultimately they are in control, and in some way a fantasy of total omnipotence is satisfied."

"Anxiety about death is common to everyone. It seems possible that one of the excitements of the spectator in motor racing is seeing someone take considerable chances, going to the limits of their own skills, and seeming almost invulnerable. It is this that reassures."

The study, undertaken in the course of a clinical investigation of a driver who had suffered a severe head injury, almost certainly Stirling Moss following the accident at Goodwood which ended his brilliant career, revealed another characteristic, namely a racing driver's ability to improve his performance under stress. Reaction times of the drivers tended to be little faster than those of non-racers, but under pressure the racers' reaction times improved, while those of control subjects lengthened.

The analysis also suggested that racing drivers did not take time to enjoy a full social life and could be unexpectedly independent of the relationships extroverts are assumed to need. Instead they affected the facade or took on the behaviour of an extrovert, even though they might be nothing of the sort.

Jim Clark's conversion to extrovert behaviour and complete compliance with the psycho-analytical model occupied most of his time in motor racing between about 1960 and his death eight years later. The metamorphosis was in some ways incomplete, but by and large the psychologist's appraisal was correct. He may have been superficially extrovert but he was inwardly repressive to an unimaginable degree. When he began racing and rallying in the 1950s he was a normal, reserved, uncomplicated person with a keen curiosity about cars and competition.

It was the happiest time of his life and he recalled the pure enjoyment he obtained from it. The heat of competitive motoring could involve getting lost in a field with his friend and fellow-farmer Andrew Russell and failing to find a way out by feeble torchlight. He rediscovered the simple pleasure and great challenge of rallying when he took a Ford Lotus Cortina on the RAC Rally with Brian Melia in 1967.

Innes Ireland. Well aware of the dangers of motor racing.

It was a rare moment of composure. Clark's career is a story of growing apprehension as he saw drivers have accidents and suffer injury. It was a process that started with Archie Scott Brown's fatal accident in 1958. It was aggravated by the deaths of Chris Bristow and Alan Stacey at the same Spa-Francorchamps track, in 1960, and reached a climax in 1961 with Wolfgang Graf Berghe von Trips's accident at Monza in which Jim was involved and for which Italian police tried to claim he was responsible. These affected him remorselessly until by the time of his death in 1968 there is every reason to believe that he was a troubled individual.

He concealed his distress well, believing that it was a form of self-discipline. He brushed aside tragic accidents by saying he was blessed with a short memory. He was not.

If there was a flaw in the *Journal of Psychiatry*'s conclusions it was that racing drivers, "… obviously do not consciously think of death". They are for the most part intelligent individuals and while they may rationalise another's accident as a misfortune that for one reason or another was unlikely to befall them, they certainly thought about death. Innes Ireland, who preceded Clark at Team Lotus, described in a sensitive obituary on Clark how he would sometimes close his bedroom door on race morning and wonder if he would survive to open it again in the evening.

Jim Clark never forgot accidents which came about as a result of mechanical failures. Racing cars by their nature were always light and often

Zandvoort 1960, Team Lotus. Colin Chapman, Innes Ireland, Jim Clark, Alan Stacey.

The family. Jim and Susan at the back,
left to right Isobel, Betty, and Mattie.

brittle, designed to the limits of technology, stretching the bounds of knowledge. Lotus racing cars exemplified the newest techniques, and like any others with any claims to being competitive sometimes ventured into untried areas of design. The cumulative effect of accidents in which drivers lost control through no fault of their own was overwhelming. Control, remember was at the heart of the psychoanalytical appraisal, and it lay deep in Jim Clark's subconscious. Control over his life and his destiny were crucial to him and once he felt he was losing them he was like a passenger in a spinning racing car, without hope and without purpose.

In day-to-day dealings he was concerned about what his family at home thought, and when he came back in 1961 after the terrible event at Monza which led to the death of not only "Taffy" von Trips but also 14 spectators, he was beside himself with worry. He brought back a cine film which he played over many many times. His sister Betty told of the strain: "He was certainly tense. He was pill-popping. He did discuss it with the family and was sure Taffy had cut in on him whether intentionally or not." It was comforting for him to return to normal and attend the Kelso Ram Sales, where he knew nobody was holding him blameworthy for the death of his friend.

Jackie Stewart's reaction to danger was that of a true extrovert. He campaigned vigorously to make motor racing safer. He never heard Jim discuss the big accidents that affected him so much. "He never talked about the von Trips accident. He never discussed it. It was part of his defence mechanism and I think it was part of his problem. The accidents were his main excuse for not getting married. He didn't want to marry when there was high risk racing involved but even that may have been a pretence to let him escape from making decisions."

Jim Clark crushed his emotions within himself, and became more tense as the years went by, relaxing perhaps superficially when he was in a car, or enjoying in a discreet way, a celebrity lifestyle to which he took with a readiness that surprised many who still regarded him fondly as a shy farm-lad. Jim had a bouncy walk but a nervy disposition. It was a characteristic Rob Walker never saw in any other driver of Clark's calibre. Moss was never so highly-strung or nail-biting as Clark: "Stirling always

used to be cleaning his nails, or cutting them or something, but he had no nervous signs whatsoever. The only time I thought he showed the slightest sign of nerves was in his first Formula 1 race after his crash at Spa. He went to the lavatory before the race."

Helen and Jackie Stewart were close to Jim. Helen blamed Jim's insecurity for his nail-biting, yet she could not imagine what it was that made him insecure: "He had his sisters to give him confidence. Maybe when he was without them he lost confidence." What is certain is that Jim never confided his fears and worries about the dangers of motor racing to anybody. David Benson, with whom he co-authored a series of articles for the *Daily Express*, could scarcely broach the subject of danger with him. He might talk to his old friend Ian Scott Watson about accidents such as the Von Trips one, to describe what happened, but never discuss the emotions involved. He never talked it over with Helen or Jackie Stewart or Jabby Crombac, or Sally Swart, or any of the journalists. He kept it to himself throughout, brooding, worrying, keeping the lid on a cauldron of emotions that surfaced only rarely in brief off-the-record moments when he could contain them no further.

Jim Clark probably did not want to worry the family. Peter Hetherington found Clark, "… a good solid Scotsman, and this charm that he had only took you so far. If you pushed him the shutters went down and you were not going to shift him. He never talked about the dangers of motor racing except to take them into account as a sensible client."

So, with reservations, Jim Clark fitted the psychiatrist's model perfectly. At the wheel he epitomised the difference between driving a racing car fast enough to achieve the back row of the starting grid, and going an extra mile-an-hour faster to gain the front. Many drivers were able to shave a couple of seconds off a lap time by grit and determination, bravery even, but the last half a second was beyond all but the talented few. The pole position's decimal digits, gained cooly, relatively safely and above all consistently, were only within the grasp of Fangio, Nuvolari, Ascari, Senna, Moss, Stewart, and Clark on a regular basis. Pole was rarely

Cloth cap, cardigan, stick, and all eyes on the sheep. Kelso Ram Sales.

achieved with courage; bravery was not enough. Even heroes of the track seldom attributed their success to heroism. Quite the reverse.

Clark's was a measured and carefully honed proficiency resulting in a rare ability to absorb the feel and noise and sensations of a racing car, understand them, and slow the action sufficiently to act appropriately. It was like driving on a knife's edge and just about as precise, not so much taking the same line through a corner lap after lap, as taking the right line through a corner lap after lap, and if there was traffic in the way, being able to vary the line to suit changing circumstances.

Jim Clark could even take account of a changing car. At the Monaco Grand Prix of 1964 the rear anti-roll bar came loose, creating a handling problem that would have had most drivers either making for the pits or slowing down. Not Clark. He not only kept his lead, but adjusted his driving to suit his car's shortcomings. Once again he fitted the psychologist's pattern, improving his performance under stress — self-imposed stress, but stress just the same. Here, behind the wheel, he felt in full control of his car, his race, and his destiny.

He had made an uncharacteristic error on his first lap, brushing against a barrier at the chicane on the harbour-front. There was no apparent damage to the car, so he pressed ahead hotly pursued by his great friend and rival Dan Gurney in a Brabham. Clark blamed himself for his first-lap blunder, and steadily improved his lap times as his fuel tanks grew lighter from 1min 40.7sec to 1min 35.7sec. It did not seem to matter that the roll-bar now had no steadying influence on the rear springing. He carried on as though nothing had happened, and it was only when commanded into the pits to remove the bar lest it become completely detached and cause an accident, that he fell back to third place. He never did manage to win at Monaco.

Former Lotus mechanic Dick Scammell, later racing director at Cosworth Engineering, was there. "His lap times dropped back a little while he sorted it out," he recalled. "But then he went back to his old times. We were not sure what the problem was, and I went down to the hairpin to see. The second time Jimmy came round after I got there, he picked me out of the crowd and gave me the thumbs up. He had accommodated the changed condition of the car within a lap and carried on as if nothing had happened."

"Beaky" Sims counted his adaptability a major asset. "He had an ability to adjust to any situation, even when the car was wrong and there was no time to put it right."

Mexican Grand Prix, 1962.

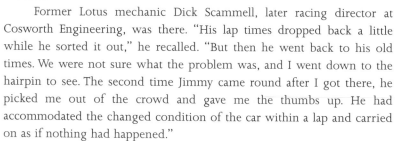

Second of four brilliant wins at treacherous Spa, the 1963 race in torrential rain.
Michael Turner's evocative painting shows Clark leading Carel Godin de Beaufort (Porsche)
on the approach to La Source.

In the Italian Grand Prix at Monza, 1967,
Clark eclipsed every driver, every car, in one of the
most dramatic races of modern times.

There was one respect in which Clark could apparently contradict the psychiatric archetype. His competitiveness was never in doubt at a professional race, but elsewhere the gentler side of his nature would reassert itself. Enjoined to publicise Scalextric model motor racing, he was beaten by wide-eyed schoolboys who would bask forever in the glow of having once defeated Jim Clark. In a famous milk float race on the Scottish track at Ingliston near Edinburgh he made a real milkman's day by sandbagging his way to second place. He had nothing to prove by bullying his way to the front. Everybody knew he was the world champion. He knew he was the world champion, but knowing he could give one Edinburgh milkman a chance to tell his grandchildren he had vanquished Jim Clark, somehow mattered more than finishing first.

Magnanimity like that showed how complete his self-control was, yet how perversely he played it out to gratify the deep longing he had for control of his car, and his life.

Clark's insouciance at the wheel had its disadvantages. When he tested a new car or a new feature, his minders allowed him only a few laps at a time because his towering talent automatically compensated for almost any shortcoming of his car. He could then be incapable of contributing useful information to the engineers because he would merely neutralise the car's deficiencies by re-calibrating his driving. Other drivers would demand changes to the suspension or the shock absorbers or the tyres or the gear ratios, but unless a car was thoroughly uncompetitive Clark, often to his engineers' despair, would set a fastest lap and say, "Fine – leave it as it is." Colin Chapman acknowledged that Clark scarcely ever used his entire reserves of mastery.

"His ability was so much greater than he ever revealed. He hardly ever drove to the limits of his capacity, He only used nine-tenths of his talent, which makes the gulf between him and other drivers even bigger."

On some occasions, like the 1962 German Grand Prix on the Nürburgring when he forgot to switch on his fuel pumps, Clark did drive at ten-tenths. Once again he blamed himself for a mistake. He was annoyed, and induced the psychological stress that drew on reserves enabling him to drive to the commanding heights he seldom needed to call upon. He was the consummate practitioner. He made it look easy, yet his sporting manners were so impeccable that he never lost control of them. Chapman was able to articulate the views of his fellow drivers. "I have never heard a word of criticism of Jim Clark's driving technique or his methods in a race."

Strain gauge. Post-race shower will wash away grime.
Haunted aspect ineradicable.

If he was at the wheel of a competitive car or, as happened from time to time an uncompetitive or deteriorating car, he was still twice as likely to win as finish in the first six. He was adept at winning against the run of play, and even though his triumphs at Indianapolis (second in 1963, victory in 1965) were the stuff of legend, his greatest race was perhaps one he did not win.

In the Italian Grand Prix of 1967 he led, lost a lap in the pits, and then caught up the entire field by overtaking every other car, some twice. It was an unimaginable accomplishment unique in modern grand prix racing. Effectively he raced a full lap ahead of everyone else up till the last lap when his car faltered for lack of fuel. It was an astounding display in an era when cars were closely matched and races decided in terms of a few seconds, on a circuit famous for close racing and yards-apart finishes. Once again Clark displayed that enormous faculty he had for self-control: outwardly calm, inwardly burning with a source of energy that improved his performance with every peak on the graph of indignation or frustration or whatever his motivation was. These were the occasions when he was able to show the world just how much ability he held in reserve, to the despair of his competitors.

Monza was nearly a famous victory, but his fuel pumps failed to collect the final few gallons in the bottom of the tanks. At first he blamed Colin Chapman, and after the crowds had stopped mobbing the winner, John Surtees in a Honda, and himself as the moral victor, he rounded on Chapman for miscalculating the fuel required for the race.

His soaring adrenalin level left Chapman the victim of a tongue-lashing that revealed a side of Clark rarely seen in public. Ten years before when the Berwick and District Motor Club had, as he saw it, cheated him out of a proper acknowledgement of his skill, he had had to defer to its authority. Now the authority was his and Jim Clark was very, very cross.

Monza and the Nürburgring were virtuoso performances worthy of Juan Fangio, Tazio Nuvolari, Rudolph Caracciola, Ayrton Senna, Stirling Moss, or any of the elite of great drivers with a natural, almost mystical

talent that exalted them to a class of their own. Walter Hayes, the Ford vice-president who played a key role in Clark's career, said at a gathering in Edinburgh to mark the 25th anniversary of the accident at Hockenheim: "He shared a birthday with Johann Strauss and Albert Einstein, and gave us a new kind of music and a very different theory of relativity."

He still bit his nails (he said it was better than smoking) and there were years of repression to come, for the rest of the world of motor racing was still full of keen-eyed youngsters certain from childhood they were going to be world champions. James Hunt was one who made it, but hundreds more never came close despite their confidence. Many, long after it was clear to everybody else they were not going to make the grade, lived out their dreams in club races either disillusioned that they had been dealt an unfair hand, or convinced that but for ill-luck, they would have been recognised like Jim Clark for their native skill and charm.

Modern biographers can be amazed or infuriated, because the person that they had regarded as a hero, great writer, great explorer or sportsman turns out to be less than perfect. It can irritate them when they find a hero who does not absolutely conform to their preconception of him, and the fact that Clark was this introverted perennially uncertain person may not accord with the popular myth.

Motor racing lost its innocence when Jim Clark died. He grew up during the war. Many of his older fellow-racers in his formative years at Charterhall or club events up and down the country were former servicemen like Jock McBain, to whom motor racing compared to anything they had been doing between 1939 and 1945, probably seemed tame, secure, and even safe. Its dangers were beyond dispute but to true followers they were surmountable – if you had the rich skill of Jim Clark.

His reputation is secure. In the years since he died there has been no muck-raking, no reappraisals, no skeletons have emerged from cupboards to sully his reputation not only as one of the greatest-ever racing drivers, but also as an engagingly modest and agreeable individual.

No longer unknown, Chapman invites Clark to drive for Lotus.

Kilmany, Fife, Jim Clark born in room upstairs to the right.
Farmhouse and Clark family home until 1942.

EARLY DAYS

Jim Clark had enormous affection and respect for his parents and his family. They were role models to him for his conduct, sense of propriety, and even morality. It was a close family which required much of him and, according to Sally Swart, Jim sometimes felt they expected too much. Still, he was careful in the way he dealt with things and always tried to give the right impression at home. Sally was among the friends who learned to be careful not to intrude on sensitivities.

Jim Clark was born on March 4, 1936, the youngest in a family of five and the only boy. His father, James Clark Senior, farmed Wester Kilmany in the village of Kilmany that lies on the main A914 leading nowadays to the Tay road bridge and Dundee. In 1936 the only Tay bridge was the one replacing the ill-fated railway structure that collapsed so spectacularly in 1879.

Kilmany nestles among low rolling hills in the north of the kingdom of Fife; a vernacular term, for it never was a kingdom. It was sporadically an earldom and a dukedom, never a kingdom despite being self-contained, with the Tay estuary on the north side and the Forth to the south. Forty miles long and 20 wide, the Fife peninsula is undulating, nowhere higher than the 1,713 ft (522m) summit of the Lomond Hills. To the east stretches the North Sea, and a sandy coastal fringe encompassing St Andrews, a bishopric in 908, a burgh in 1140, seat of Scotland's first university in 1412 and the home of golf. To the west lies Loch Leven, Perth, and the Ochil Hills reaching a modest 2,363ft (720m). Assertions by Fleet Street or American television that Jim Clark was a species of romantic Highlander had little foundation. In 1942 when he was six, he moved to the Borders, to Berwickshire and another farm barely half a dozen miles from England, and almost within range of the salt spray sweeping in off the North Sea.

James Clark Senior was ambitious. Wester Kilmany had been mixed with both crops and animals, and he bred sheep and fattened cattle, mostly Irish and generally good stock, but in poor condition when they came from the same Dublin family his father bought from. It was a trade based on confidence; neither side would take advantage of the other; not only would it have been a shame to spoil a good business, it would have dulled a long-standing friendship.

James and Helen Clark discouraged racing, yet were proud of world titles. Jim fretted constantly over their "understandable anxiety," and threatened to boycott Indianapolis.

Trust and confidence were essential to the Clark family culture.

His father's generation had been through the first world war and the depression of the 1930s. Born in 1897, James Senior had been brought up to sheep-rearing, looking after lambs when he was 12. At 17 he joined the Fife and Forfar Yeomanry, trained in Suffolk, was drafted into the Black Watch, a kilted regiment, and sent to the Western Front. He trudged through the trenches, and had bitter memories of the wretchedness and the rain, and the French turning off the water supply, leaving soldiers parched, dirty, and starved. He never forgave the French for that.

He survived the slaughter, but in the dying months of the conflict, during the winter of 1918, he was captured near Cambrai and imprisoned in a coal mine near Essen. The Germans treated him well although his diary revealed that Red Cross parcels were a vital increment to his meagre diet. The family kept relics of his experiences, including a dictionary given him by a guard so that he could learn German. He also had the complete works of Robert Burns, much of which he committed to memory. It was fully a year before he was fit enough to return to farming.

Jim's grandfather put up money for a hill-farm in Kinross-shire with spectacular views towards Loch Leven. It was an impressive 1,000 acres. Hill-farms were large and an adjoining one was duly bought for a brother, leading to family rivalry over sheep at agricultural shows in Kinross and Perth.

In June 1924 he married Helen Niven (born in the south of Fife in 1900) after a year's engagement, but by 1931 he had had enough of hill-farming and moved east to become tenant of a farm belonging to the Anstruther-Gray family at Kilmany House. He was now an arable farmer which meant new disciplines, but was so successful that he took on three more farms. His achievements owed a lot to good agricultural machinery: he was accomplished when it came to machinery.

It was a long and happy marriage. James was outgoing, talkative, and enjoyed meeting people. Helen was hospitable, kind, but retiring, although when the occasion demanded she was an expert hostess. Both had lots of relatives whom Jim's sisters were constantly welcoming. One sister described her mother as thrifty, even though she sometimes cooked for 20 at weekends. Helen's father had butcher's shops, went into farming, and became provost of Inverkeithing in 1911. He sent Helen to school in Edinburgh for a time, for which she did not much care.

Not long after his parents and elder sisters, Mattie, Isobel and Susan, moved from Kinross-shire, Jim's sister Betty was born at Kilmany, and 3½ years later the future champion driver of the world arrived, to the delight of James Clark Senior. Girls were all very well and their parents loved them dearly, but here at last was an heir. Walter Hayes ascribes some of Jim's character to the close family bonds: "It was a matriarchy up there. Here they were all hopping around perfectly lovely, beautiful thrushes or robins and then all of a sudden there was this flamingo thrust into the middle of them."

Jim Clark Junior was born into a deep-rooted Presbyterian culture where deception was as alien as bad manners or cheating at Bridge. It was not strict; there was no need for that, but they all grew up with a clear idea of what was right or wrong, fair or unfair. It was all part of a deep-rooted Presbyterian ethic, a moral code created for the guidance and well-being of small agrarian communities in a northern land with not many people.

The farmhouse at Kilmany was square, stone-built, set back from the road, with farm buildings ranged alongside and to the back. To the left of the large front door a sitting room was reserved for visitors. On the right was a living room and a large dining room with a huge table to accommodate friends and relations who thronged the house. Back rooms off the kitchen included maids' bedrooms, while upstairs there was a large bathroom, a guest bedroom, and three more bedrooms. The stairway divided, providing access to yet more bedrooms above the front door which the family occupied in different combinations at different times. They had to double up when air-raid evacuees arrived from Glasgow.

It was a spacious house and a happy home. Betty and Jim had a nurse to look after them, and there were two resident maids in the back. Family gatherings were frequent, large, and noisy, and holiday exchanges took place with cousins and friends, often for long periods in summer. Father was conscientious, hard working, and as eldest in a family of nine of whom four were younger brothers, felt a responsibility to do things properly. Punctilious and dependable, he admonished those who were not.

A Kirk elder at Kilmany, James Clark was also elected session clerk, a

Son and heir at last.
Jim with nursemaid and sisters Isobel, Betty, Susan.

key post in the committee which ran the church, from 1931 to 1942. Session Clerk was a lay Church of Scotland appointment and led to a family joke that Jim was nearly baptised James Session Clark.

Jim's sister Betty believes their father had a strong, quiet, Presbyterian faith: "I suppose reserved Scots don't talk about it much but he was a regular churchgoer." When the older sisters attended Sunday school, she accompanied father. "He was an elder so we had to go early and I climbed onto the pew and waited for the others. Mother was there when she was not busy preparing Sunday lunch."

James would travel a long way to obtain good prices for cattle and sheep, and on one journey to the Borders found Edington Mains Farm near Duns. He looked it over, and closed the deal within days. It was not a sudden impulse: he thought the Merse of Berwickshire, the fertile plain north of the River Tweed, was one of the best agricultural areas in Scotland. To farm there had been a long-cherished ambition; farmers from the north and west still come to the Borders in search of fertile soil and a calm climate. It is one of the sunniest parts of Scotland, although an east wind blowing across the North Sea from Scandinavia could bring an icy chill or blow a wet haar well inland.

Edington Mains. Well-tended lawns and graceful aspect of Jim's home until he emigrated in April 1966.

Jim Clark went to the village school in Kilmany with sister Betty. Isobel was at school in the next village, while Mattie and Susan were old enough to take the train to Dundee High School across the silvery Tay of William McGonagall's immortal poem. Their father bought Edington Mains in May 1942, but it was the first week of August before the family moved. Susan was 14, so she and Isobel went to Berwickshire High School.

Jim and Betty walked or cycled to the primary school at Chirnside, where they were bright pupils at the astonishing art deco building looking more like a suburban Odeon than a small country seat of learning. Built in the 1930s it was something of a local landmark of which the small border township was exceedingly proud.

Art-deco in the Borders. Chirnside school, a smaller edition of Kelso High School, and within walking distance of home.

Edington Mains had a dozen or so cottages occupied by farm workers, and a further six elsewhere, so there were plenty of local youngsters at school with Jim and Betty. They played robust school games, sledged in winter and skated on a pond that froze in the chill northeast wind.

Jim was competent at organised sports; Betty said he had a good sense of balance, and he was quick and agile. He usually beat her at table-tennis on the big mahogany dining table. When visitors came he would join in a boisterous game of French cricket, or tennis on the broad Edington lawn. For serious tennis they cycled the short distance to a grass court at Edington Mill House where he played well apart from a tendency to cricket-style strokes. Rainy days meant cards or Monopoly which went on for hours. In summer there were long talks, dogs to walk, and animals to tend. As childhoods went it was a country idyll; short on stress, long on strong family bonds.

Jim remained at Chirnside school until, as the clouds of war lifted and confidence returned, he and Betty were sent to boarding school. Jim went to Clifton Hall, a preparatory school near Edinburgh from 1946 to 1949, Betty to St Hilary's, evacuated in the war from Edinburgh to Thirlestane Castle at Lauder, with other Border girls.

Jim started at Loretto School in the winter term of 1949, by which time St Hilary's was back in Edinburgh, so outings with mother in the capital usually included both children, and Betty remained close to her brother. Jim enjoyed music, they went to orchestral concerts in the Usher Hall where Betty recalls Alexander Borodin's epic Prince Igor, with its resounding Polovtsian Dances among his favourites. He was a member of the Loretto choir, took part in a performance of the St Matthew Passion, and once, to his mother's surprise, sang a solo on Sunday in Chapel.

When he appeared on *Desert Island Discs* with Roy Plomley in 1964 his choice of records was expansive, ranging from the melliflous Glasgow Orpheus Choir through Chris Barber's *Whistlin' Rufus*, Billy J Kramer, and Jimmy Shand's Scottish Dance Band. Andy Stewart's *Muckin' o' Geordie's Byre* reminded him of the farm and Peggy Lee singing *The Party's Over* perhaps of romantic nights in faraway places. He also chose an excerpt from humourist Gerard Hoffnung's famous address to the Oxford Union, and

Bach's *Sheep May Safely Graze* which the school organist at Loretto used to play as a voluntary after evening service.

Loretto was a profound influence. Private education was, and remained, rare in Scotland which was one reason I concluded at that first meeting in Edinburgh in 1955 that the Clarks must be well-off. Scottish education is traditionally civic, with 96 per cent of the population state educated. Of the remaining 4 per cent, most attended public schools close to Edinburgh. It is worth remembering that the equivalent in South-East England was around 14 per cent or more.

So Jim started life in a privileged section of Scottish society at a venerable institution with roots going back to 1820. Its buildings included Pinkie House near the scene of the battle the Scots lost against Henry VIII in 1547. There was more bloodshed at nearby Prestonpans in 1745, and Pinkie House was used as for the casualties; the bloodstains of the wounded are still visible in The Long Gallery. Prince Charles Edward Stuart, Bonnie Prince Charlie spent two nights there in the room once occupied by the young King Charles I, before entering Edinburgh.

Bill Cormie, later an amateur racing driver himself, shared a dormitory with Jim Clark at Loretto, and remembers him as a very private person. "He was very self-sufficient. He had few close or special friends. He really was quite taciturn but we did share an interest in cars and I was extremely jealous when he came back after half-term and said he'd been driving at 90mph. We didn't believe him of course. He was only 14."

Loretto was a strict school in the 1950s; less radical or experimental than Gordonstoun established in 1934 it nonetheless had similar aims of character-building and good citizenship. It believed firmly that conformity to well-established rules was an essential part of good behaviour.

Jim Clark, age 16. Final year at Loretto. "I was no great scholar…"

The school motto: "*Spartan nactus es: hanc exorna*" means literally "You have achieved Sparta: adorn this". It was more generally translated as "You have acquired the privilege of living like a Spartan: show by your example that you have something worth having."

Loretto's pupils were drawn from professional and military homes, civil and foreign services, farming, and industry. Cormie remembers many who came from wealthy families: "There were others whose parents were making real sacrifices to provide a 'good education.' Yet money or lack of it never affected school attitudes, and if

Loretto in the 1950s by Scottish artist W K Henderson shows Clark's father's Alvis, school uniforms.
Boys wore ties only on most formal occasions.

there were any cases of hardship, the authorities ensured that it never showed."

Loretto's day began with a cold bath for every boy immediately after their 7 am wake-up call. Summer or winter they immersed themselves in cold water over their shoulders in large cast-iron tubs; masochists would sit and splash it over their face and hair, but most managed to be in and out in seconds brooking no delay for the orderly queue of naked shivering bodies. Smart boys learned to judge the surge of water in the bath, leaping in to the shallow end and springing nimbly out again before the wave swung back. If his timing was right the water only came up to a boy's waist; if it was wrong, he was in it up to his neck.

Dormitories varied in size from four to over a dozen boys, headed usually by a sixth former. Prefects had their own rooms and were allowed hot tubs in the morning, run for them by third or fourth formers. Prefects could turn up for breakfast ten minutes late, drink coffee instead of tea, smoke a pipe on Saturday evenings, and take shortcuts across the grass. They wore long grey flannels and went around with jacket buttons undone.

'Fagging', the public school practice of junior boys running errands and doing menial jobs for older ones was forbidden. All boys regardless of age had duties to do for a week or two at a time however, like clearing the tables in hall, bell-ringing and so on.

In the morning after roll-call "links", was a 10 minute jog round the old Musselburgh racecourse and golf links. Meals were taken at long tables, some with 40 diners, with a prefect at each end then sixth formers and so on down to third formers in the middle. Pupils gradually moved to the end of a table, which meant first pickings for the older ones and short rations for third formers.

Breakfast was always porridge, something cooked like a fried egg or sausage, and a floury roll. Most boys supplemented this with their own jam or marmalade kept in nearby food lockers.

At 9.55 the whole school had headmaster's assembly or "double" – so called because to get there in time you had to run at the double. This would consist of announcements, a short Bible reading and a prayer. At 10.15 it was back to the classrooms for three more lessons with a 10 minute break for milk and biscuits. Sixth formers were exempt from gym and did 40 minutes wood-cutting for the school fires instead.

After lunch there was another "double", this time the Head of School's, with announcements on sporting matters or on the school club meetings. At 1.50 there was one more class, followed at 2.30 by a

compulsory period of sport or exercise, rugby in the autumn and spring terms, hockey in the spring term and cricket in the summer. If all the pitches were occupied exercise was still compulsory, and anybody who had not arranged fives, or tennis – or more wood-cutting – was obliged to run five to seven miles. Hot tubs were taken after all exercise, followed by another cold one.

Sports and games were an important feature. The school believed that life was competitive and everyone had to participate. There was little clemency for weak or fat boys. Some of the runs were timed and failure lost the house points. No one was spared the 940 yard 'Newfield Course' which had to be covered in a set time for each age-group.

At 4 pm came "small tea" – a quick visit to the dining hall for a slice of bread and a piece of cake or a biscuit, then two more 40 minute classes and "big tea," something cooked, with plenty of bread and jam supplemented by whatever was in the personal food locker.

Prep began at 7 pm sharp. Every pupil up to the fifth form had to be in the Colin Thomson Hall for 90 minutes under the duty master. Set prep was divided into three periods of 30 minutes, and talking was strictly forbidden.

There was a free period at 8.30 for club meetings, fives or tennis, play rehearsals or playing musical instruments. Boys were free to visit the art room, workshop or library, or just wander around and talk.

Finally, at 9.10 pm came another Head of School's "double" in the dining hall, where there would be a short Bible reading and a prayer. The school then went to bed every night except once a week when each room had a tub-night. This was a hot bath (followed of course by another cold one) which was very welcome when the north winds blowing in off the Firth of Forth chilled the dormitory. Throughout the school in any room where boys were present the windows always remained open.

Discipline was by self-regulation through the prefects who constituted a sort of internal police force. Offences were common and often quite minor, like failing one of the regular book or food-locker inspections, general untidiness or walking on the grass. Most serious would be missing official exercise. Punishment was called after "big tea" with miscreants despatched to the big tubroom, where a prefect would deliver a minimum of three strokes of the cane on the backside, up to six if the offence was unusually serious. Canings were received wearing white shorts which were usually thinner and worn to emphasise the disgrace. There was only one "six in whites" administered during the time Clark and Cormie

Decorous Clark at 21. Jim remained faithful to a well-cut suit, tie,
and often a wooly pullover or cardigan throughout his life.

Home of the brave.

were there. Masters would also dispense classroom punishments, mainly for academic slackness.

Shopping was allowed in Musselburgh on Saturday half-holidays, but not within 200 yards of school, and only at approved shops. A deep suspicion was harboured by the boys that the school obtained better terms from the favoured establishments. It was about the only time boys mixed with the community.

Big sporting fixtures were played on Saturday afternoons, and when they were against other schools it was compulsory to watch. Exercise was prescribed for everybody afterwards, usually a short run. If there was no cricket match in summer, bicycle rides could be taken and self-catering picnics were popular, with the proviso that no shopping could be done within the first five miles. There was no prep on Saturday evenings but a one hour singing practice for the chapel services next day.

Sundays meant an extra hour in bed, and no "links". Apart from a scripture lesson and two services in the school chapel, it was a day for relaxing and writing home. Leave to go out with parents was granted three times a term between morning service and evening chapel.

"We knew we were a privileged and selected lot," said Cormie. "There was little mixing with the local community. Yet there was no attitude of superiority, probably on account of the strict regime at Loretto. You got on better if you were both sociable and competitive and while this may be instinctive to some, others were largely left to fend for themselves."

"The school probably did not generate a healthy attitude to girls. During term time girls were almost a race apart and something of a mystery – especially to those who did not have sisters. As you got older there was great ogling of other boys' sisters when they visited. The only occasion girls were admitted to the school unattended was at the end of the summer term when the sixth form ran their "shirt-sleevie" – a dance in the gym where all boys wore open-necked white shirts and white shorts – and girls were conducted off the premises afterwards."

Jim enjoyed Loretto. He liked sports and, although perhaps he failed to embrace academia wholeheartedly, he was by no means backward. He did not specially excel at schoolwork, remaining consistently in the C stream, but neither was he slow, idle, or mutinous. Betty said: "I can't think what he was best at; he would be middle-of-the-road at most things, and although no swot he certainly was not bottom of the class."

He never laid claim to much scholarship and declared his reports contained remarks such as: "He could probably be quite good if he would put his mind to it." He played rugby, cricket, and hockey, and allegedly did not understand what use Latin was going to be for a farmer. Jim's chief sport was still cricket. He had "naturally quick reactions" according to his brother-in-law Ken Smith, a Scottish rugby international.

There was a perversity in the way Jim played down his scholastic capabilities. It may have been by way of explanation for his lack of formal qualifications, which he may have found embarrassing in a motor racing world full of intelligent, highly-motivated, and highly-qualified individuals. It abounded in well-educated technicians and inventive graduate engineers such as Colin Chapman. Yet Jim may have been doing himself a disservice, and although he often said he was indifferent to lessons and got into trouble through playing truant, he was quick-witted, intelligent, relatively hard-working, and certainly no delinquent.

Perhaps the real reason he disparaged his good education was to relieve his father of any obloquy which might have arisen from removing him from school in 1952 at 16. It was, after all, done to suit the family business, and Jim may have been more sensitive to leaving school prematurely than he appeared. He once said he left when his father realised he was not studious, but there was something faintly apologetic about his assertion that: "Father had no qualms about taking me away from school. He thought I would learn more on the farm than I would from school books."

The reason for quitting Loretto was a family crisis. His uncle and grandfather died within a fortnight of one another, and the succession had to be settled. Jim was plucked out of school, given responsibility for Edington Mains, and as soon as he came of age was taken on as a partner in the family firm. Following the deaths, James Clark Senior ran three farms. In addition to Edington Mains, he took over Kerchesters for his father's trustees, and Over Roxburgh for the trustees of his brother, all three remaining in the family. James Clark Senior was responsible for Kerchesters, Jim's cousin (yet another James Clark) ran Over Roxburgh, and Jim took control of Edington Mains.

It covered 1,240 acres with a further 200 acres of woodland. It had between 700 and 800 breeding ewes,

Autumn, 1965. Following father's operation for gastric ulcer Jim and his mother visit Edinburgh nursing home. Jim nearly gave up racing awaiting father's recovery.

Precarious existence. Jim balanced life on the farm against that
of a world champion racing driver. Even in 1963 he could still be found
among the sheep.

three pedigree flocks; Oxford Downs, Suffolk Downs, and Border Leicesters, and fattened around 500 cattle a year for sale in local markets. There were usually about 500 acres under the plough, on which the Clarks grew barley, wheat, oats, potatoes, and turnips.

Had he not left school so early he might quite easily have gone to college to do engineering for which he seems to have had an aptitude. During school holidays Jim moved cattle, tended sheep, and looked forward to harvest time with the family. These were days before combine harvesters mechanised it, and there was keen competition to see whose haystacks would withstand bad weather when it came. He became entrenched more firmly in farming, although the ambition to dabble – it was no more than that – in motor sport had taken root at school.

Billy Potts, Jim's cousin who was to enter motor racing history by supervising the future champion's first adventure at 100mph, farmed nearby. "The Clarks were a well-respected farming family. Jim's father and his grandfather were very good farmers. They paid attention to detail as far as the stock was concerned. They were meticulous in buying the best possible, without paying over the odds. They liked to do things the right way."

Leaving school was a turning point, although the implications may not have seemed profound at the time. After all, Jim had been preparing to be a farmer all his life and he had a fine self-confidence about it. He knew he would not be short of advice on how to do it. The family was nearby, his older sister, Isobel, was to run his household and he really wanted to get on with what he had trained and prepared for since childhood.

Betty felt he had other reasons for welcoming the respite from school. "It meant that he would be driving his own car, and soon. He had been driving since he was nine years old, he liked the country, and he knew a lot of people in farming." Jim became a member of the Young Farmers Club which ran motor gymkhanas, and he began to get a taste for the world outside school.

Yet his tidal wave of enthusiasm for cars nearly broke on the unyielding disapproval of his father. Jim's nature and outlook was heavily influenced by his father. When his father fell ill, Jim came home often, even when duty-bound to continue motor racing into 1966. After he won his first world championship he talked at length with his father about retiring. Colin Chapman persuaded his favourite driver to stay on, and although James Clark Senior wanted Jim to come back to the farm, he gave grudging approval because he knew Jim's heart by now lay firmly in motor racing.

Clark's smile filled the frame.

EARLY DAYS

Jim's father passed on his knowledge of farming, business, finance, animals, and the rotation of crops. His mother was not fond of the girls working on the farm, but father expected them to, especially in wartime. He did not encourage the girls to ride horses because he'd had a cousin killed on one. The influence on Jim of four older sisters must have been far-reaching, perhaps creating such warmth and security at home that it led to the relative insecurity he may have felt elsewhere.

There were other influences that Jim's father passed on that were more far-reaching. The first world war played a part in James Clark Senior's somewhat stern philosophy; Jim never felt as comfortable abroad as he did at home. It was all part of that Scottishness that Walter Hayes was to find so elusive. Scotland has been called a national village, its smallness not only meant that I came to know two of the greatest world championship drivers of modern times, it created institutions different from those of England. The most important to the family culture of most Scots was probably the Kirk, not just because of the Clarks' formal connections with it, but because of the effect it had on Scottish manners and society as a whole.

The Church of Scotland in the 1990s has 800,000 communicants, or 22 per cent of the adult population. In the 1930s at Kilmany the proportion was probably nearer 50 per cent. The equivalent figure for England is 3 per cent, indicating the influence of Presbyterian ideology – not necessarily churchgoing – on almost every aspect of Scottish life and in particular on the way the Clarks, father and son, conducted themselves.

They must also have been influenced by being brought up under Scots law. That was just as much part of the fabric of Scottish society, almost undetectable but deeply rooted. The basis of Scots law is not precedents, decisions handed down by courts which are then used to guide later actions. It is a set of principles drawn up for a small and relatively poor country before the Union of 1707. Heavily influenced by Continental European scholars, Scots law did not always need to wait for a court to decide a verdict. It was theoretically possible to look up a solution to many a legal problem in a book. It gave legality to a spoken contract, and as a result Jim Clark regarded a written contract with Team Lotus unnecessary for the first two years he drove for it.

James Clark tells delighted daughters they have a brother. 4 March, 1936

Works drive for Ford.
1965 print marked Ford Motor Company Ltd, Tractor Operations, Basildon, Essex.
Sturdy Ford 4000 built 1964–1968 three-cylinder diesel of 46bhp.
Edington Mains would pay £1,500 for it.

TRACTORS, ALVIS, AND
SUNBEAM MK III

Jim's father thoroughly approved of his early preoccupation with tractors. They were an essential part of the business. Farm children often grew attached to them, as they had to horses in an earlier age. Jim's inquisitiveness about mechanical things gave him a deeper insight into racing cars than many people realised. On the farm he nurtured his interest in driving and engines; speed was not at this stage important but movement was. He took every opportunity of getting behind a wheel, learning as much about tractors as the regular farm drivers. He felt it was part of the job and there was still only one job. Farming.

Motor vehicles, cars, vans, or tractors were still not much more than a means of getting from place to place, and his mother had quite given up driving before the move to Edington. Clark Senior ran an Austin Seven during the war, having decommissioned his Alvis Speed Twenty. Multiple car ownership was still unusual in Britain, but farmers often set a big car or van aside for the duration of the war; its petrol ration enabling them to drive farther in something smaller and more economical.

The little side-valve Austin was the first car Jim Clark drove. He was nine. Like most mechanically minded boys he could see how it was done, he was accustomed to tractors, so off he went by car, round the rutted farm tracks. It was not quite so easy when the Alvis was dusted down and brought back into service in 1946. Jim Clark was not tall. Even when he was grown-up he was only 5ft 7in and 150lbs, and to get the big Alvis with its long bonnet and huge headlamps on the move he had to press the clutch pedal, select first gear, let the clutch out and jump up on to the driving seat in order to see. After that it was easy to steer and control speed with the hand throttle.

Unfortunately, reversing out of the garage his sleeve caught on the hand throttle control and before he could dive back under the scuttle to reach the clutch and brake, a wall intervened. The Alvis was strong, the damage did not amount to much, and he kept the first accident of his driving career secret for years.

Guests at a family occasion noticed the Alvis apparently driverless leaving home. Father had to explain that it was Jim, completely invisible from behind, and he would be back soon. His first paid driving job at sixpence an hour was on a tractor at harvest time. He was still only 10.

The farming apprenticeship extended to sheep and cattle sales and grain markets, the novelty of which soon wore off. Sales tended to start early in the morning and continue until late afternoon, often ending with the day's dealings and prices being discussed in the bar while Jim waited outside.

Just as he began full-time work, one of the shepherds left so Jim's father gave him a dog and a stick and told him to take over. Sheep-minding was never going to be his career, but in farming as in any other family business, members of the family were expected to turn their hand to anything. Shepherding would provide good photo-opportunities in years to come, although portraying Jim Clark as a shepherd who became a world champion driver was to misrepresent the facts. Perhaps posing with shepherd's crook and cloth cap was but a small deceit.

Family snap of Clark at Kelso Ram Sales.

It probably seemed harmless enough to play along with the press, although it was inconsistent with the misgivings Jim had about his portraiture in Scotland after he entered motor racing. He saw nothing contradictory about being represented to the world as a shepherd which he patently was not: he simply did not take it seriously. He dismissed it as a Fleet Street gambit, even though he was at pains to conceal any hint of racy living from his homelanders. He was more concerned about the reactions of his father and his immediate family than the adoring fans he gathered as world champion.

It shows the pressures he created for himself that it led to a life on twin tracks. Duplicity? Not quite. It was more like dual control; two levels of existence, one a relaxing mode at home on the farm, the other a high-pressure, dangerous, and demanding business, and keeping them apart was like having two mistresses. It was safer and more comfortable to keep them separate. One was allowed to take peeks at the other; his sisters went to grands prix, his friends came back to Edington, but the contacts between the two were superficial except in one area which, in the end turned out to be unfortunate to say the least.

Up till 1960, Jim's parents encouraged Ian Scott Watson to accompany their son to European races. They felt happier knowing a friend was with him. He had plenty of friends when he was racing with the Border Reivers; the entire team was composed of them, but when he turned semi-professional they still wanted somebody with him in case of emergencies. James Clark had never quite overcome his distrust of the French and he was not too sure about the Germans. It was always better, surely, to have somebody you knew nearby rather than have to cultivate new comrades and new advisers.

The Scott Watsons were a farming family with little enthusiasm for cars. Ian was six years older than Jim and, like him, brought home from school before he finished his final year, after his father took ill and an uncle died. He administered three farms with about 50 employees and in terms of financial nous and worldly awareness was well ahead of the younger Clark.

Scott Watson passed his driving test in the family Wolseley 12 in 1948, with petrol rationing still in force, after driving for a year on a provisional licence. He had wanted to take the test earlier but there was not much opportunity to practice driving except on essential business. He knew the Clarks as neighbouring farmers with a reputation, like all Fife farmers, of being financially astute.

He shared an M-type MG with his brother, and used his first competition car, an MG J2 for rallying. This was followed by a TC and then a Buckler. He had wanted a Lotus Mark VI but did not trust Colin Chapman enough to part with his cash. He sold the Buckler with relief instead and bought his first DKW.

Ian went to Winfield, an old airfield circuit six miles from the farm, to watch Giuseppe Farina drive in one of its first international meetings. Scott Watson's mother lived near Northampton, so he also went to Silverstone for the 1949 Grand Prix, the second big race it ever staged. In 1953 at Ednam Young Farmers Club he forged the friendship that launched Jim Clark's spectacular career.

Giuseppe Farina (in hat) set fastest lap at Charterhall in October 1952 driving Thinwall. Clark and Scott Watson watched 1950 world champion at Scottish track.

Inspiration for Jim Clark. The sight of Ecurie Ecosse C-Type Jaguars on the road stirred motor racing ambitions. Jimmy Stewart leads Ian Stewart at Charterhall in April 1953.

Clark's enthusiasm for motor racing was ripening. He had read the three books on motor racing in the school library at Loretto and was avidly scanning motoring magazines. The arrival of the weekly *Autosport* became a special occasion, particularly after his eldest sister Mattie married Alec Calder (of the racing Bentley and Riley) in 1948.

Clark's first sight of real motor racing turned out not to be in Scotland at all, but at Brands Hatch in Kent. The track was in its original kidney shape, without Druid's Hill, or extended grand prix circuit. He was taken there as a treat by relatives living nearby and found motor racing exciting, faster than he had imagined, yet curiously uninvolving. He bought an autographed photograph of Stirling Moss more as a souvenir than because of any fascination with racing drivers, for he was far more interested in the cars.

Unlike Scott Watson he had not been to races at Winfield, yet motor racing seemed to seek him out. On his way home from a cricket match at Jedburgh he encountered three C-type Jaguars driving towards him on the winding, undulating, well-surfaced roads near Kelso. The big sports-racing cars in the dark blue livery of Ecurie Ecosse were braking heavily from high speed, darting about the road as the drivers held them in check. "Peculiar," thought Jim, but felt a twinge of envy.

When he heard that Ecurie Ecosse was testing the Jaguars at Winfield he cycled the six miles, and climbed through a fence to watch. He said he dived into the undergrowth when challenged although he does seem to have made contact with the team. The first motor race he saw in Scotland was at Charterhall, a few miles south of Duns, Berwickshire, in October 1952. It had a star-studded cast for a small meeting in remote Scotland with Giuseppe Farina from Italy driving the Thinwall Special against Johnny Claes, the Belgian band leader, in a Talbot, and the Siamese prince B Bira in an OSCA. Stirling Moss was in motoring writer Tommy Wisdom's C-Type Jaguar with the new disc brakes, and Ian Stewart beat him in a similar car belonging to Ecurie Ecosse.

The driving stars still did not catch Jim's imagination and even Farina, the first champion driver of the world, did not impress him. It was the stub exhausts and calico-tearing noise of his 4.5-litre V-12 Thinwall Special that transfixed the schoolboy who would one day eclipse the cool Italian aristocrat whose first competition was the Aosta St Bernard hill-climb in 1932. Farina raced under the tutelage of the great Nuvolari. Ironically he lost his life in 1966 at the wheel of a car made famous by Jim Clark, a Lotus-Cortina.

When he turned 16, Jim asked his parents for a motorcycle with predictable results. They would have none of it, probably wisely. The Nortons and Triumphs and BSAs of the time may not have been as fast as the Hondas and Yamahas and Kawasakis of a later era, but one regular rider in 20 was dying or being seriously injured. Had they acquiesced, Scotland might have had to wait until Jackie Stewart for its first world champion.

Jim Clark took out a provisional driving licence as soon as he was 17, and passed his driving test six weeks later. It was his key to freedom on the fast and relatively traffic-free roads of the Merse with their long corners and good sight-lines. His sisters had a 1½ litre Riley

Ecosse drivers Jimmy Stewart (left) and Ian Stewart in cars, Bill Dobson stands behind. Charterhall, 1953.

to use in Edinburgh, and his father switched to Rovers. When the first Rover arrived, Jim took over his father's Sunbeam Mark III with 12,000 miles on the clock.

His father had a stubborn streak too. He refused to be budged from the Rover even after Jim forged firm links with Ford. Walter Hayes: "Old Jim was a serious and a much respected father and you didn't talk too much at the dining table. He was very rigid in his ideas. When Jimmy joined Ford, we tried to get his father out of that Rover. He absolutely wouldn't. I offered him a new tractor but he didn't really want a new tractor because his old tractor was doing very well thank you."

In 1954 the Sunbeam gave Jim status. It had a strong affinity with motor sport, and the Sunbeam-Talbot rally team had been one of the most successful in Europe. In 1952 Stirling Moss, Desmond Scannell and John Cooper drove one to second place in the Monte Carlo Rally. Moss was already well-established, Scannell was secretary of the British Racing Drivers' Club, and Cooper (no relation to John Cooper of Cooper Cars) was sports editor of *The Autocar*.

Bill Boddy, veteran editor of *Motor Sport*, tested a Sunbeam Mark III in 1955 and reported, "...this rather heavy and old fashioned saloon sprang a very pleasant surprise. It handled extremely well, was devoid of vices, felt and proved to be 'unburstable' and was capable of averaging 60mph at the expense of a rather startling rise in fuel consumption ... a rugged and handsome car ..."

Boddy's 'unburstable' was a generous compliment. It was a code-

Cloth cap, racing number in sticky tape, draught deflector still in place.
Amateur motor sport at its happiest. Jim Clark in the Sunbeam.

word to readers accustomed to eulogies on Volkswagens, to describe the Sunbeam's low-revving refinement. A Norwegian crew won the 1955 Monte Carlo Rally in a Sunbeam Mark III which confirmed young Clark as something of a connoisseur where cars were concerned.

It was not quite like that. Connoisseurship was not likely to have carried much weight with James Clark Senior, although he liked a good car, and the Sunbeam was stylish and swift albeit not large. Its top speed of 91mph, and 0 to 60mph acceleration in 18.4sec was at the lively end of the performance spectrum in 1955. The four-cylinder 2.2-litre engine was an overhead-valve conversion of the Humber Hawk, and for a time the only ohv engine in the Rootes range, but its steering column gearshift was scarcely appropriate for a budding world champion.

The column shift was not the Sunbeam's only American-influenced feature. Appliqué styling included wide chrome grilles flanking the radiator, and three 'portholes' like a Buick, designed to mimic the stub exhausts of wartime fighter aircraft.

The Sunbeam's flowing wings and rakish air were probably more appropriate to Clark Junior than they had been to Clark Senior, although a rake at this stage he certainly was not. Girls were still something of a mystery despite, or perhaps because of, having grown up in a household full of them, and it was largely through the Sunbeam that he made an impression at the Ednam and District Young Farmers' Club, where the next piece of his career jigsaw fell into place.

Meeting Ian Scott Watson not only provided Clark with his first racing cars, but his new friend encouraged, persuaded, and would effectively suborn him into the Lotus grand prix team. Ednam and District YFC could be said not only to have brought Scotland two world motor racing championships and two more near-misses with Clark, but arguably, through the part played in furthering his friend's progress, also the three more titles and two close-calls that followed with Jackie Stewart.

Much, as Samuel Johnson observed, may be made of a Scotchman if he be caught young, and Ian Scott Watson, small, wiry, brimming with ideas and energy, was a motoring enthusiast who had the fortune and the foresight to catch Jim Clark young. Scott Watson drove in rallies, he had the means to indulge his obsession, and he loved motor racing with almost evangelical fervour. He wanted everybody to share in the great world of motor sport, preaching a gospel of speed to people living near the borders of the north of England and south of Scotland.

Almost as soon as he became a licensed driver, Clark took part in the

Berwick and District Motor Club's autotest meeting at Winfield. Autotests were for standard road cars, the competitors timed through tests which involved a dash to a line, a reverse into a garage, perhaps a spin turn, and a dash to another line. Accuracy and precision were more important than speed, and the cars varied from family saloons to sports cars; nothing fancy, it was essentially amateur.

Jim enjoyed flinging the Sunbeam round pylons, discovering once the results were added up he had been declared a winner. The bad news was that he was disqualified on the grounds that he was not a member of the Berwick and District Motor Club.

He was not best pleased. He had a special dislike of being deceived or cheated of success, and the canny outlook that distrusted anybody outside his immediate circle asserted itself. His indignation was a little unjust; competitors were expected to be members, and the officials had little option but reject him. Nevertheless he felt slighted and for some time refused to join the club, taking a wry satisfaction from being awarded honorary life membership after becoming world champion.

By the 1950s motor sport was losing some of its upper-crust image, and once the boundless zeal of the motorcycle racers was enlisted after a financially disastrous international meeting in 1955, its commercial success became more credible. There was now a real prospect of motor racing in the Borders.

Racing drivers' careers have crowning glories and crushing failures, and Jim Clark's had its share of both. Chief among the depressions were those created by his own self-doubt. His early years were punctuated by crises of confidence engendered partly by his place on the farm where his prospects could scarcely have been better or more secure. He was desperately worried that he might not be very good at motor racing, or that he might look foolish. And since his upbringing made him suspicious of people outside the family, obtaining a second opinion was difficult.

Among friends, in particular Scott Watson, there was little doubt about his potential, and every step he took on the driving ladder was marked by distinction. He passed every test of aptitude and proficiency, progressing from gymkhana to autocross, then to rallies, and finally racing. He began with Scott Watson's modest two-stroke DKW, then small sports cars and then big sports cars. He moved to single-seaters in the novice category of Formula Junior before graduating into Formula 2.

First he competed in local rallies, fearful that his parents would proscribe them on grounds of expense. As far as Clark Senior was concerned, rallying was a waste of a good car and Jim's Sunbeam cost more to run than the Rover. Bill Boddy's conclusions about heavy fuel consumption when driven fast were near the mark.

Yet even parsimonious parents could not object to him taking part in rallies as a navigator or co-driver. The 1955 International Scottish Rally was not like its successors, with rough-and-tumble special stages for reinforced cars. It was organised by the Royal Scottish Automobile Club (founded 1899), whose grand headquarters were in Blythswood Square, Glasgow.

Scottish Rallies were gentle affairs, sometimes scoffed at as social events. RAC regulations prohibited average speeds over 30mph, so they had declined gently and elegantly to touring assemblies, with the competition confined to autotests, or sprints and hill-climbs. The 1955 Rally comprised 1,200 miles of fast motoring on roads not only without speed limits, but often without traffic. It was an opportunity for keen young drivers to go fast. Nobody was expected to run late, and of the 105 cars that took part in the last week of May 1955 not many did.

It was a blissful week. The sea at Oban shimmered in a heat-haze. Billy Potts, Jim's cousin, needed a stand-in for his regular co-driver, and the pair set off in Potts's Austin-Healey 100. It was four minutes late on the first day's drive to Oban which earned Clark his first mention in a motor sporting report. Still only 19, he savoured a tour that showed Scotland at its magnificent best, to parts of the country he had never seen before and sadly never saw again.

It was not a good event for the happy farmers of the joyously titled Ecurie Agricole. One member, Johnny Somervail, crashed his week-old Austin-Healey 100S at Snetterton and, after hitching a lift in an aircraft belonging to Ron Flockhart, set off in his old car instead.

Ian Scott Watson's navigator Alan Curry was marooned by a rail strike, and Ronnie Dalglish blew the exhaust gasket of his Triumph TR2 half an hour before the start. He joined Potts in a Glasgow garage where he was having the brakes fixed. Curry overturned Scott Watson's DKW and finished the rally with a crumpled roof.

There was nothing sombre about Glencoe in May 1955 when Potts handed over to his young co-driver. Jim Clark took the wheel of the low blue Healey, driving gingerly past the scene of the massacre of 1692 when Campbell of Glen Lyon and his soldiers slew 40 Macdonalds. Jim's competition licence was just three months old. Potts knew they had plenty of time: "We were moving along well, when another Healey went past. That was too much. As the car went faster I said, For God's sake, canny Jim,

Scottish Rally, 1955.
W K Henderson depicts Bill Potts and Jim Clark (Austin-Healey No 111) on the "Little Rest",
with Frank Dundas and Eric Dymock (Morgan Plus Four No 103).
Royal Scottish Automobile Club official is A K Stevenson.

steady. But within minutes I relaxed. All the ability was already there. He was an absolute natural. He had the car completely in his grasp."

It was the first time Clark drove at 100mph.

He navigated on rallies, but not well. Scott Watson said he was impossibly bad, with no sense of direction, and on one tightly timed "plot and bash" event where the navigator had to work out the route quickly, he became exasperated by the folds of the map and spread it out on the back seat. But kneeling on the front seat shouting instructions made lefts into rights and led to confusion.

It was decided thereafter that Jim should drive.

Yet even as the "Scottish" was winding its relaxed way round the Highlands, Scott Watson was preparing Jim Clark's first tentative step towards motor racing. Clark found driving the Sunbeam on grass exhilarating at an MG Car Club autocross at Romannobridge between Peebles and West Linton. The car was constantly sliding, and his skill soon showed.

Perhaps for the first time, his remarkable sense of balance or keen eyesight or the sensitivity that gave him exquisite control of a racing car was exercised. It was at 50mph, not 150mph, but it had all the sensations he would feel on the track in slow motion. Controlling racing cars by a combination of steering and throttle control was a technique all but gone by the time Jim's career came to its abrupt and tragic end.

The "four wheel drift", analysed by Stirling Moss and the technical writer Laurence Pomeroy, to explain how Farina and Fangio and Ascari drove, would pass into history. By the 1960s tyres made of sticky substances giving phenomenal grip made it unnecessary. Jim Clark never drove a racing car with wings providing downforce to claw the tyres into the tarmac, which also changed driving techniques in the years ahead.

Meantime, the four wheel drift was something a budding racing driver had to master, and the emergent Clark found the experience absorbing. He appraised it carefully, but having been brought up to regard modesty a virtue, he was shy about ascribing mastery of it to his skill. "You can throw the car sideways and see if you can get it back again," he enthused. "You can experiment in safety in a way you never could anywhere else. Autocross is like racing on a skid-pan."

Clark's early exploits with Austin Seven caused consternation.

First race. Jim Clark at the wheel of Scott Watson's DKW, No 4.
The starting grid of a career that will include two world championships and
a record tally of Formula 1 victories.

CRIMOND 1956

A year passed before Clark took part in his first real track event. In June 1956 Ian Scott Watson entered his DKW Sonderklasse for a race meeting at Crimond in Aberdeenshire, and Jim went along ostensibly as his mechanic. Scott Watson had ridden often enough in the Sunbeam to be convinced that Jim had a rare talent. Crimond – the tiny Aberdeenshire parish that gave its name to the tune of the 23rd Psalm composed either by the minister's daughter or by an admirer and named in her honour – witnessed the beginning of a new vocation.

The meeting was run by the Aberdeen and District Motor Club. Scott Watson's car, a new one since the Scottish Rally accident, was used for rallies, sprints, and gymkhanas, and he entered for the sports car race and the handicap saloon car race.

The DKW was neither a sports car nor a very competitive saloon. It was a small two-stroke with a lineage going back to the 1930s and although it revived the old Auto Union name and four-ringed symbol, the first car built in the bomb-damaged Rheinmetall-Borsig plant in Düsseldorf was based on a design dating back to before the war. It had a transverse two-stroke twin-cylinder engine, and a body intended for a 1940 car except that there was no scuttle-mounted fuel tank and the fuel feed was by a mechanical pump instead of gravity.

"Motor racing is dangerous…" Bland injunction applied to next 12 years.

DKW's traditional backbone chassis was abandoned in favour of a box-section frame, and the rear suspension was by a transverse spring and axle beam. To reduce the heavy two-stroke fuel consumption it was rounded off for better aerodynamics with flush headlights, and a long tail enclosing the luggage boot. It was only eight inches (20.3cm) from ground to floor, and 57 inches (144.7cm) tall.

By 1950 the DKW was better-engineered, carefully detailed, and when it was re-styled in 1954 with a big bay window at the back, it gained a revised three-cylinder engine known as 3=6 (three cylinders with the firing impulses of a six-cylinder: a German technical quip). The new F91

Sonderklasse had an 896cc engine developing 34bhp, a roller-bearing crankshaft, and a four-speed gearbox.

This was the car that set Jim Clark off on his great career, but why should Ian Scott Watson choose an obscure and rather smoky German two-stroke costing £948.17s.6d, when there were more obvious saloons like the MG Magnette ZA at £914.17s.6d or sports cars such as the Austin-Healey 100 at £1,063.12s.6d or Triumph TR2 at £886.10s.10d (£943.4s.2d with a hardtop)? Clark's Sunbeam Mark III was £1,127.7s.6d and the Alpine, which might have been a logical option, £1,212.7s.6d. The new Ford Anglia was making a name for itself with good handling and roadholding despite its rather weak 1,172cc side-valve engine, and cost a mere £511.2s.6d.

The reason was that DKWs had form. The 1954 European rally champion Walter Schluter, and runners-up Gustav Menz and Heinz Meier drove them. A DKW won a Coupe des Alpes for a penalty-free run in the Alpine Rally; another came third in the 1956 Monte Carlo Rally, and won the Safari. Scott Watson knew a DKW had qualities to score outright Scottish rally wins not only against Renault 760s, Standard 10s, Morris Minors, and Austin A30s, but also beat established sports cars.

It was a long drive from the Borders to the windswept disused airfield at Crimond eight miles from Fraserborough. In 1956 before the Forth road bridge, the northwesternmost tip of Aberdeenshire was nearly 250 miles away, and in a small two-stroke car took five hours.

The runways at Crimond made an agreeable little circuit, and in an effort to even out the small entry, the organisers awarded handicaps based on practice times. Sandbagging was prevented by a penalty clause invoked if race times exceeded practice times by too great a margin.

Scott Watson secretly filled in an entry form for Jim to take part in the sports car race. There was a practice session in which Clark proved three seconds a lap quicker than he, which confirmed what Scott Watson had suspected, namely that Clark had more ability than he knew. It did not prove he was going to be three seconds a lap faster than everybody, because Scott Watson was experienced, skilled, knew the car, and was not three seconds a lap below par.

The conspirators discussed the situation. They were far enough from Berwickshire for Clark's family not to know, so they decided to take a chance. Scott Watson's persistence won through, Clark conceded, and lined up on the starting grid.

The emotions surrounding his first race were memorable. He felt the

Ian Scott Watson fostered Clark's start in motor racing right up
to Team Lotus and first years in Formula 1.

track was hallowed ground. Racing had become a sort of holy grail; he had no chance of winning, but he was in a crisis of anxiety in case he made a fool of himself.

Jim was so much quicker than the car's owner that there did not seem much point in Scott Watson racing again. He did not yet know what was involved in organising Jim's career, but he was convinced that here was a potentially great racing driver and determined to give him every chance. He was quite prepared to do it on his own if necessary.

For the time being at any rate, his motives were altruistic. Scott Watson loved motor racing and although he had been ambitious as a driver, once Clark's ability emerged he saw himself in the role of promoter. He was the first to provide a car, and took the initiative in advancing Clark's career.

Jim still worried about his aptitude. It was part of the real modesty that went with his upbringing, his family, his school, his Scottish, not to say his provincial, candour. He worried about accidents for the good practical reason that if he had one and damaged the car, his parents would be bound to hear about it. It was only later that he worried about accidents because drivers were hurt.

He took a lot of motivating. He did not realise how good he was and Scott Watson spent the first years encouraging him to believe in himself: "I may not have been a judge of what was required to make a grand prix driver, but I could tell from the way Jimmy drove both on the road and on the track that he was exceptionally good. On the road he was amazing, perfect to sit beside. His driving was smooth, and his anticipation marvellous. You could feel him ease off the throttle and then spot a car he had already seen approach on a distant side road. It was difficult to know why he did not feel confident about his own ability. He chewed his fingers even then. He lacked confidence, yet when he got on the track it was totally forgotten. He gave it everything and drove superbly."

Clark not only drove well on the track, he drove successfully on rallies, in driving tests, hill climbs, and later in sports car races. The moment he got behind the wheel and the flag dropped, his worries were dismissed, yet his mentor had to make a huge effort to get him there in the first place.

In the race at Crimond he had been surprised to overtake one car until he discovered it had broken a half shaft and was dropping out. He finished last, but he had been introduced not only to motor racing but also to officialdom. Scott Watson was hauled up before the stewards, accused of

deliberately slow driving in practice, and was rehandicapped out of contention in the saloon car race.

When Jim Clark began racing there was little occasion for his family to discourage him. The likelihood of anybody British aspiring to be a professional racing driver was, for the time being at any rate, remote. Motor racing, like bullfighting or fomenting revolutions, was for the most part something foreigners did. The Italians were good at it, and so were the French. The Germans had been magnificent in the 1930s and again in 1954 and 1955, but when Jim Clark was a schoolboy there were few British cars and scarcely any British teams in the top flight of motor racing. Jaguar provided some shafts of sunlight with sports cars at Le Mans and when Ecurie Ecosse inherited the previous year's works cars and won twice it was the stuff of dreams. But that lay in a remote future world.

In Formula 1 the BRM raced fitfully but proved fragile and temperamental. Until the later years of the decade only Vanwall could provide an amateur with the material to fantasise about Formula 1.

Driving a racing speed-boat or flying your own aeroplane were also so much in the realms of fantasy that it is unlikely Clark's parents felt any need to discuss them, far less discourage them. The perils of playing rugby or driving up the A68 to Edinburgh were more real. Motor racing never cropped up until Jim's brother-in-law Alec Calder dabbled in it much as friends dabbled in the Hawick Common Riding every June, to commemorate a bunch of local toughs who roughed up some English soldiers in 1514. Motor racing would surely be much like a sporting ride round Hawick, giving young callants a chance to show off.

The Jim Clark legend that he received scant encouragement from his family was not quite true. He got time off to go racing although not much practical support, yet he never bought a racing car in his life, and sponsorship was scarcely the structured business it became. It was perhaps not encouragement he needed so much as permission for what probably seemed a self-indulgence: like Common Riding or yacht-racing or competitive ski-ing. By the time professional motor racing became a serious option for Jim Clark, it was too late to talk him out of it.

The future champion grew up in a family that could afford to indulge him a little, and he enjoyed an agreeable car. "He was born with a car in his mouth," as Walter Hayes put it. "And it was a sporting car in his mouth." In terms of fortune or private income the family did not regard itself as wealthy. Its members were certainly hard-working, but holidays were not carefully structured affairs at hotels, and there were few real

Formula 1, 1960s style.
Casual group on the infield at Brands Hatch includes
Esso racing manager Geoff Murdoch on right, Jim Clark with camera,
Sally Swart, beside her South African Cooper' driver Tony Maggs and,
on left newcomer Jackie Stewart.

extravagances. In material terms they were not badly off, and in the security of family love and affection they were indeed rich.

Jim was expected to take up farming and in due course run one of the family farms. There was no compulsion. There was no need. Jim himself happily expected to take up farming. It was fulfilling, it would provide him with a good living. His sisters could have taken it up had they wanted to, but they were not expected to want to. They might marry farmers as they were likely to in the social whirl around Young Farmers' Clubs and the lively lives of four attractive and intelligent girls.

Farming sons were not tied to the business totally. Many of them enjoyed sporting hobbies like rugby, a Border obsession with a lively tradition of providing the amateur backbone of the Scottish international XV. They were not expected to carry on playing indefinitely of course. Why would they want to when they could farm?

This was Jim Clark's cultural background, and he became deeply concerned about his absenteeism during the early days in motor racing. He still saw himself as indulging his hobby, and for races that took him away during the working week, he took the equivalent of his annual holidays. He was not seriously embarking on a career as a professional sportsman. Even after he was engaged to drive in Formula 1 he still did not think of it as a career. True, it was not quite like Alec Calder's amateur races in his classic little Riley, it was further up the scale than that, even though the main difference was that instead of paying to go motor racing, somebody else paid him to do it.

Maturity in motor racing meant taking time off from the farm. Becoming a professional sportsman was a distant prospect for Jim Clark.

It was not possible to earn much, but at least it kept the family off his back if he could retort: "Look, it's not costing me anything, and I expect I will come back to the farm next year when it all stops." His situation was rather like that of a student who "takes a year out" before going on to the next stage of education. Families put up with it even if they really feel it is self-serving dallying.

Jim Clark never signed up with anybody for long because it kept his options open. By the time he was world champion and heavily committed to motor racing, he was unwilling to opt out because he was enjoying it.

Colin Chapman and Lotus were relying on him, and Esso and its racing manager Geoff Murdoch had invested heavily in him. Getting out of racing then would mean letting somebody down.

It still did not look like professional racing to James Clark Senior. Jim may not have been spending his own money on cars and preparation – they were being subsidised by Scott Watson and McBain – but the cost to the Clarks was mounting and, like any family subsidising sport, the expenditure was scrutinised.

Jim was becoming addicted to racing driving. He truly loved it. He had the time of his life in a racing car and later perplexed one American television interviewer who speculated that: "The appeal of money is certainly not the lure of your type of racing?" Jim said, "I would probably still race, maybe not in Formula 1, but I would still race even if nobody had ever paid me anything. I started out with no idea of ever making money at it, and it was only at the beginning of 1960 when my father got a bit upset that I was spending so much time racing and suggested that his hobbies always paid for themselves that we began to look seriously at the possibility of making mine pay as well."

It would have been no different had it been skiing, riding, sailing, or bobsleighing: time and money would have come under review. The young Clark still never imagined that he would be a professional sportsman. His family regarded motor racing as a dilettante activity, like show-jumping or yacht racing; all very well if you could afford the equipment, but more likely to be a pursuit of landed gentry than farmers.

In due course Ford and Walter Hayes would invest in him too, and by 1965 he could no longer walk away from it even if he wanted to. His sense of loyalty went deeper than his agrarian family roots and, up to his emigration under pressure from the Inland Revenue in 1966, he still felt he could pick up the traces again if it ever became necessary.

Choice of this sort was a rare luxury for a country boy on the one hand and a professional sportsman on the other. Either way he was not going to be badly off, and it explained why he never quite embraced the ideology of the modern professional racing driver with all that meant in hustling, making deals, endorsing products, writing newspaper articles, opening supermarkets, and dealing with the press. He regarded these as tiresome, little to do with motor racing, nothing at all to do with farming, and mostly unnecessary.

It was one of the paradoxes of Clark's life that much of his apparent insecurity and seeming indecisiveness stemmed from this feeling that

somehow motor racing was a temporary phase. It was too good to miss, but it was not real life. Sooner or later he would settle down, perhaps back at the farm, perhaps with some sort of business interest, perhaps in conjunction with the man who became his mentor, his master, and in the end his undoing, Colin Chapman.

He isolated his temporary motor racing life from his steady job as a farmer. He may have quite enjoyed posing for publicity pictures at the Kelso ram sales or Edington Mains, reassuring his friends at home that he had to play along with the foolishness of it all. His staunch support locally was heartening and he quite liked the respect he gained from his family and friends from knowing he excelled. He found being acknowledged as the best in the world curiously comforting, together with the knowledge that he did not actually need to be a farmer. Conversely it was consoling to know that he did not need to be a racing driver.

He worried that his family would think him boastful about his ability, concerned that his lifestyle appeared flamboyant. He was anxious about it not just because of his Scots background and upbringing, but because of the strong influence of his father. He also wanted to exercise the option to return to normality if he should choose. Some saw James Clark Senior as a tough uncompromising character and while James Clark Junior might not have agreed, the culture into which he was born saw to it that airs and graces had to be kept in check if there were to be any hope of a peaceful after-life at Edington Mains.

Early in Clark's career a journalist turned up at Monaco with a photographer in search of stories about girls who followed grand prix racing; Clark warned him to be careful what he wrote. He was only allowed to accompany the party on condition that he did not portray Clark's life as extravagant. "People in Scotland read your magazine in doctors' and dentists' waiting rooms. I don't want them to think that I live a jet-set life in Monte Carlo all the time."

Yet he did want them to know he was a success. He found it satisfactory that people knew he was a winner. That way he still felt in control at least among those who mattered to him, and to whom he did not want to appear self-important. He was never above putting people in their place, especially anybody inclinded to scoff at the idea of a local boy making good. After winning his first title he wrote: "A lot of people who thought I was a young idiot came up to congratulate me. Half of Berwickshire, it seems, predicted that I would one day be world champion."

One result of what a later age might have regarded as complacency was that he failed to make the money in motor racing that he deserved. It was only his victory at Indianapolis that brought him much wealth, and even then it was scant in terms of what drivers of the 1990s could earn. Jim Clark's total career earnings probably did not exceed £1 million. In 1968 when Jackie Stewart was earning around £100,000 a year, the double world champion may have been making less.

Still, it represented real wealth for somebody who did not like talking about money. Indianapolis was one of the few occasions when he did admit to thinking about it: "Every lap I was in the lead I could see dollar signs."

Otherwise money was something of a taboo. Ian Scott Watson never talked about money with him throughout their friendship, neither during the early years when he organised Clark's races with the Border Reivers or later when he was racing professionally. "The Reivers prize money went to him and the starting money to the owner of the car. It was an informal arrangement." Jock McBain, who also sponsored the Reivers, and Scott Watson spent more than they ever got out of it. "Neither of us resented one moment of it, and when Jimmy died he left me a small legacy which certainly recompensed me for what I had done."

One of the reasons Jabby Crombac remained friends with Jim was that he was careful never to mention certain topics, among them money. "I never said a word about it and never borrowed a penny off him. The word money did not exist between us."

Clark's unconcern with money meant he passed up opportunities for product endorsement. He put his name to kangaroo-skin driving gloves and supported Scalextric slot car racing when he won his first championship. He was also connected with driving shoes but that was about it.

The *Daily Express* was confident he would win Indianapolis and negotiated a deal for him to write a five-part series. He was paid between £250 and £300 for each one, a total of perhaps £1,500 (£14,900 at 1990s prices) with world serial rights and some share of syndication income, but it was not a lot for a major sportsman and a world champion even in the 1960s.

When Ford signed him up, nobody knew what it was worth, and his retainer of £5,000 (less than £50,000 in the 1990s) was modest. Clark did not seem to understand that there was much more money to be made out of motor racing in the way Stirling Moss did. He was more interested in gaining publicity for motor racing as a whole, perhaps remembering how

Scott Watson struggled to bring motor racing to the Borders, and still feeling the sport needed promotion.

Jackie Stewart never understood how Jim could be so casual about money. An oil company retainer could be worth about £20,000 in the mid-1960s. In 1968 Stewart felt he had the edge on Jim. "I don't think Graham Hill was earning as much as we were. Probably I was earning more than anybody else. Jim was quite well off but he must have seen what other people were earning. A top executive at the time was getting maybe £10,000 or £20,000 but not £100,000."

Jackie felt he had had an influence: "I think I got him to recognise values. We started differently. I didn't have any money, and Jimmy was quite rich by comparison. I didn't have that advantage, and I wanted to be able to buy my own house. Jimmy already had a house with his own house-keeper."

Stewart thought Jim Clark was probably naïve when it came to money: "There's no question. Not just in money but in a lot of other ways as well." Helen Stewart believed he did not lack for anything, although he occasionally appeared mean. "We would go out for dinner and normally split the bill, but Jimmy would prefer to pay exactly for his bit. He would say what he had had and apportion it out."

He may have been a giant in the cockpit but outside it some quirks of character sometimes showed up. Graham Gauld found one when they were doing a book together and he visited Jim at Edington. "He had a little room which he used as a kind of office and hanging in a cupboard he must have had 25 jackets. They were mostly quilted jackets with racing logos. A lot of them were American. We were all young and enthusiastic, and impressed, I said to him that I'd love to have one. But he wouldn't let me. He said, 'Oh well, I might need them in case I've got to do an appearance or something …' "

The psychological need to feel in control of events was a strong feature of Clark's make-up, and the apparent indecisiveness referred to by many of those who knew him was probably superficial. They all experienced frustrating excursions looking for restaurants, or witnessed dithering over money or girlfriends. Yet he was never indecisive in a racing car and many of those with whom he did business found him inflexible to the point of stubbornness.

The farm lad's graduation from tractors to a funny front wheel drive car did not go unnoticed.

TKF 9, the Border Reivers' D-type Jaguar as restored by Bryan Corser.
Eric Dymock drove it at Oulton Park for an Autocar feature of 20 June 1968.
"...good manners... perfect balance."

MILESTONES IN MOTOR RACING
AND TKF 9

Scottish motor sport in the 1950s was dominated by Ecurie Ecosse, into which Jim Clark did not fit. He was invited to drive only once and his co-driver crashed, but by then the slight was unimportant. He had made his way in the world without Ecosse, and the omission only rankled because it cast doubt on his ability during the critical years when his greatest battle was with his own self-confidence.

In Scotland's motor racing community an endorsement from Ecosse was important, but like Archie Scott Brown, who was well into the "gifted" category alongside Moss and Hawthorn in the middle 1950s, Jim Clark never hit it off with Ecurie Ecosse's founder, David Murray. "Although I know and like David Murray very much indeed," Clark wrote. "We never seemed to agree in racing. There was friendly rivalry between the Border Reivers and Ecurie Ecosse and as a Reivers man I thought I should never drive for the opposition, although David did promise …"

He was being kind. When he dictated that passage to Graham Gauld in 1964, Murray was still at the head of the team, respected and admired for sustaining a small private and ostensibly amateur outfit that had beaten the professionals twice in the Le Mans 24 Hours race. Once would have been an achievement: twice was unprecedented.

Jim Clark and David Murray (right) founder of Ecurie Ecosse.

David Murray's enthusiasm was kindled at Brooklands in the 1930s. After the war he raced ERA R12B "Hanuman" with David Hampshire. Enthusiastic rather than proficient, he beat Reg Parnell, then a leading driver, at Winfield in an old Maserati. He obtained a 4CLT/48 like Parnell's and came sixth in the Ulster Trophy, two laps behind Farina the 1950 world champion.

Murray crashed in practice at the Nürburgring effectively ending his career, although whether through a promise to his wife or awareness that he was probably not going to make the grade we may never know. Instead he assembled customers of the motor tuning business he had set up, and offered them a team management service. They would own the racing cars, but as a team they probably commanded better starting money than they could as individuals.

The sleek Ecurie Ecosse Tojeiro-Jaguar at Goodwood,
September 1959, wrecked by Gregory.

Three young men wealthy enough to own XK120 Jaguars pooled their resources and Ecurie Ecosse took to the tracks with Ian Stewart, Bill Dobson, and Sir James Scott-Douglas. Ian Stewart drove for the Jaguar works team, and could have gone on to greater things. Ironically Jim Clark regarded him as "a highly strung person, and yet at the wheel he seemed as relaxed as anything". What a mirror image of himself.

Ecosse became responsible for the later C and D-type Jaguars, financed partially by Murray's wine and spirit businesses, but mostly by the enigmatic Major Thomson, shipping magnate, vintage car collector, and recluse. The eccentric Major wanted Scotland internationally recognised in motor racing, and his gifts to Ecurie Ecosse included most of its cars. Murray wrote to him almost daily but in secret. A stipulation of Thomson's philanthropy was that nobody should know of his involvement.

His great fear was of injury to a driver.

In the 1961 Le Mans race, Bruce Halford crashed the team's Cooper Monaco, and its prototype Austin-Healey Sprite suffered a similar fate. Halford was not seriously injured, but Bill Mackay, a young Scottish driver in his first big race suffered head, neck, and arm injuries. They were the most serious of any driver in an Ecosse car, and it proved too much for Major Thomson.

David Murray sustained a certain stylishness. An Edinburgh chartered accountant, businessman, and entrepreneur, he had a feel for motor racing that made him at best a visionary, at worst a gambler. He won Le Mans and the hearts of his fellow countrymen more than once, yet died in exile, out of credit on the race track as well as at the bank.

Murray wanted Scottish firms to finance a team for international sports car racing, but with a vexing indifference to their overseas prestige, the canny Scots kept their purse strings tight. He set up a supporters' club with which in the end, he fell out, yet he recognised the commercial possibilities of Can-Am and other forms of racing 10 years ahead of Bruce McLaren, and 20 ahead of Bernie Ecclestone the modern ringmaster of Formula 1. Like Colin Chapman, he regarded presentation as crucial, he pursued publicity, and his drivers agreed to paint their cars the same colour. Gleaming, confident, professional-looking, the Ecosse cars glistened in flag metallic blue and set new standards for private teams everywhere.

It was not enough for David Murray. The team had no income, and customers did not flock to the garage at Merchiston Mews, near Morningside, Edinburgh. The wine businesses were sold or mortgaged, and as they were neglected they became worth less to sell or raise money on. The cash ran out, and with his creditors closing in, Murray escaped to the Canary Islands, but once again, his luck ran out. He died of a stroke in 1973 following a minor traffic accident.

"It was the only time his courage failed him," wrote the *Scottish Daily Express*. Why it should fail him in his native city, so profoundly, after a lifetime in accountancy was a mystery.David Murray's obituary on Jim Clark was curiously cautious: "I did not know him well, in fact during his lifetime I can recall having only two long conversations with him, but there sticks in my memory the sight of a schoolboy cycling from his home to Winfield when Ecurie Ecosse was testing its Jaguars. Even at that time he was keen on cars, intelligent in his questions about them, enthusiastic and shy." Faint praise from the man who scorned Clark in his early years.

Within months of writing the obituary Murray had fled, a sad end to a career that put Scotland on the motor racing map of the world, and gave the country its distinctive motor racing colours, the dark blue and white of the St Andrew's cross flag.

Rob Walker, a scion of the Johnnie Walker whisky family, borrowed the blue with a white noseband for his racing cars, and Jim Clark chose dark blue with a white peak for his helmet.

Murray's choice of drivers was essentially commercial, and in 1953 the joining fee for an up-and-coming newcomer was £1,000, or something like £9,800 at 1990s prices. Jim Clark would have come with no sponsorship, no family cash, and few prospects. Murray professed encouragement for young Scottish drivers and took on Jackie Stewart, but by then control of Ecosse was in the hands of its well-meaning committee and he perhaps had little choice.

Ironically however, it was on his solitary engagement with Ecurie Ecosse that Jim Clark convinced himself that he was indeed a driver of quality. In September 1959 Murray invited him to drive at Goodwood in the Tourist Trophy, a long-distance race in which he would pair up with his old hero Masten Gregory. They drove

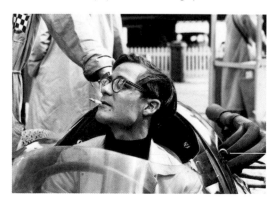

Jim Clark's self-confidence grew when he found he could keep up with Masten Gregory.

the team's Tojeiro-Jaguar and Gregory crashed it, but not before Clark realised that he was at least a match for Gregory. His lap times were just as fast. Indeed Gregory was never in his league as a driver but in 1959 Clark regarded him as outstanding. Discovering that he was just as accomplished took him up a crucial rung of the motor racing ladder. Barrie Gill: "Jimmy often took a lot of convincing about something. But once he had made a judgement, it was unswerving. After the Goodwood race with Masten he knew that he was a star driver. He never flinched from that judgement."

There was another reason for Jim's faint disapproval of Ecosse. Although its headquarters was in Edinburgh, some of its drivers, such as Ninian Sanderson were from Glasgow, and could be a touch boisterous. There were traces here of old East-West Scottish rivalries, of well-bred Edinburgh-educated folk tending to play rugby and looking down on Glaswegians whom they regarded as rowdies supporting football too noisily and much too often.

Border Reiver Jimmy Somervail racing his ERA at Turnberry Ayrshire, 1953.

One of Ecosse's principal sponsors was Esso, whose competition manager Geoff Murdoch spent more than £100,000 a year on racing. There were retainers for drivers and bonuses for winning, and free fuel and oil, but nothing laid down about how much went to the team and how much to the drivers. Esso did separate contracts for Jim Clark with whom Murdoch dealt directly. A strict rule laid down by Murdoch's predecessor, Reg Tanner, was never to deal with an intermediary. Jim once brought along Chris Weir, the Duns accountant to help with negotiations, but Murdoch regarded him with disdain.

The Border Reivers was the very antithesis of Ecurie Ecosse. Casual, loosely-knit, it was formed with a fine regard for autonomy – anarchy really – by Jock McBain who raced a Cooper 500 against Alec Calder in his Brooklands Riley. There was no £1,000 joining fee, but then there was no corporate structure either, no common paint job and no team orders.

It was a collection of friends rather than a focus of rich enthusiasts, with a variety of cars including an early Lotus Eleven. In 1953 it lined up for a group photograph with an ERA, an Aston Martin DB5, a Cooper-Bristol, and five Cooper 500s. The ERA was once again R12B "Hanuman", raced by Raymond Mays, Pat Fairfield, and B Bira before David Murray and

Border Reivers with loot.
From left Bobby Hattle, Ian Scott Watson, Jim Clark, Colin Clark (no relation),
Jock McBain, and Jim's brother-in-law Alec Calder.

David Hampshire. The Somervails acquired it in 1951 in time to finish second in the Formule Libre race at Turnberry on the Ayrshire coast.

McBain's influence on Clark's career was as profound as that of Ian Scott Watson, although tragically not so long-lived. A former Royal Air Force flight engineer, he was the local Ford dealer. His territory was Berwickshire and north Northumberland, but his rural garage did more than buy, sell, and repair cars. It did a healthy trade in tractors and acted as blacksmith and general engineers to the farming community.

McBain made farm windmills, and the garage was not far from Edington Mains. Jim Clark's errands to fetch tractor spares were prolonged by discussions with the proprietor about motor racing culminating in McBain offering to provide him with a proper car, on condition that Scott Watson was responsible for the organisation. The Somervails agreed to join in.

McBain's motive was sheer enthusiasm. He did not expect to make money; nobody made money from club racing, but he thought publicity for the Ford dealership might count towards the expense. He had no advertising agent and Scott Watson's job included producing advertisements for the local press.

To Scott Watson, McBain was well-educated but a rough diamond. He was good company and not only the inspiration behind the Border Reivers, but also of Winfield and Charterhall, the two circuits in the Borders where motor racing restarted after the war. Winfield was a small satellite station to the larger Charterhall, the night-fighter airfield from which Richard Hillary, author of the classic war-time biography *The Last Enemy* took off on his final, fatal flight. Its two mile lap included a seemingly endless straight on the main runway and it saw some ambitious events in the early 1950s.

Charterhall 1961. From left Jimmy Stewart now retired, Graham Birrell, Gordon Hunter, and Jackie Stewart contemplating his new career.

Ken Wharton drove the V-16 BRM, and Reg Parnell a prototype works Aston Martin DB3S at Charterhall. It was the cradle of Scottish motor racing and among the young drivers who cut their racing teeth here were Jimmy Stewart in his Healey Silverstone, attended by his teenage brother Jackie. Ninian Sanderson and Ron Flockhart, both to be Le Mans winners, raced here, and when Jackie Stewart first took the wheel to race, it was at Charterhall. In order to divert family attention, he was entered on the race programmes as A N Other.

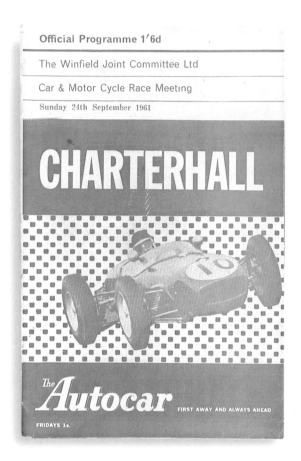

By 1961 Jim Clark featured on Charterhall programmes,
but raced less often on his home track.

July 11 1959, Bo'ness, Lister scored fastest time.
Clark drove Elite to win class the same day.

Charterhall's finances were never secure and it was only rescued from bankruptcy by the Lothian Car Club and the Winfield Joint Committee. McBain was one of the WJC's members, and it invited Scott Watson to organise a supporter's club. He persuaded them instead to form the Border Motor Racing Club (BMRC), which was inaugurated in February 1956 with Jock McBain as chairman, Ian Scott Watson as secretary, and John Somervail as assistant secretary. The competition secretary was a somewhat reluctant Jim Clark of Edington Mains.

Scott Watson wanted the Border Motor Racing Club to have its own race meetings and if the Winfield committee discouraged them at Charterhall, he would look elsewhere. He and Jim Clark set out to visit every airfield between the Tay and the Tyne, until they found Brunton Beadnell, near Seahouses in Northunberland. An unofficial race meeting was organised but the local chairman of the Lord's Day Observance Society owned a fragment of the track, and insisted it was not used for anything except agriculture.

Following the launch of the Border Motor Racing Club, Jim raced fitfully in his Sunbeam and the DKW, picking up class wins on the experimental circuit at Brunton. It was June 1957 before he took part in another speed event, a sprint at Charterhall with the DKW and September before he beat a new Austin-Healey 100/Six with his Sunbeam.

Scott Watson had the bit between his teeth. He sold the DKW and bought a Porsche 1600 Super that had belonged to Billy Cotton the band leader, entering it for the inaugural Border Motor Racing Club meeting in October. Jim Clark came third in the production sports car handicap, second in the production touring car handicap, and won the BMRC Trophy.

Another milestone was passed. It demonstrated that given the right equipment he could win. It also demonstrated that the applause for success could be unexpectedly muted. He won in Scott Watson's car at a meeting largely organised by Scott Watson (who with the RAC timekeeper Lewis Jamieson also arranged the handicapping system), promoted by a club with which Scott Watson was prominently associated. There was resentment among people who still did not appreciate the enormous new talent that was on display. The trophy race contained the leading five finishers of the other races, and when it rained Clark was the only driver to beat his handicap.

July 11 1959, Bo'ness, Porsche 7th fastest sports car under 1,600cc.

Equestrian statue feature of Border towns. Hawick's commemorates 1514 capture of Hexham Pennant from English soldiers. Galashiels horseman modelled for Border Reiver crest.

Once again he took satisfaction in being able to show in the long run that there had been no deceit, and it was all down to his driving, although he was characteristically careful to give credit to the car: "The Porsche was fabulous in the wet, enabling me to beat the Healey 100 S-types which I would not have expected to," he asserted, but he knew perfectly well that most of the success was really his.

He still regarded the Porsche as potentially lethal however, after Peter Hughes, who had driven for Ecosse and was editor of *Top Gear*, the magazine of the Scottish Sporting Car Club died in his at Ecclefechan. He was returning from the 1957 Le Mans only weeks before Jim's triumph at Charterhall. Porsches had not relinquished all their Volkswagen ancestry, were at best quirky and at worst unpredictable. The 1600S was capable of 100mph and in the BMRC Trophy race gained an entire lap on his friend Jimmy Somervail driving a Ford Zephyr.

Clark finished the season with a sprint at Winfield, but motor sport was still a hobby and, amid the petrol restrictions of 1957 that followed the Suez crisis, Scott Watson acquired a Goggomobil to eke out his petrol allowance. Jim Clark drove it in an MG Car Club autotest meeting and came second in the under 1,300cc class for closed cars. But he fumbled in the Sunbeam and took second place to a new driver who would earn respect later: works Rover rally driver-to-be Logan Morrison beat him in a Singer Gazelle.

Rallying still occupied some of Clark's time both as a competitor in the Sunbeam and also on Berwick club events, as an organiser of its famous Border Rally, a connection with his name kept alive in the 1990s through the annual Jim Clark Border Rally. Clark won in 1958 and competed again in 1959 in a borrowed Ford Anglia. He was the only competitor with a clean sheet on this notoriously tough event until he holed the car's sump. The rally was won by the Scottish Rally champion, Logan's brother Sandy Morrison, in an MGA.

He grew very serious about rallying, and his car-handling on the MG Car Club's Moorfoot Rally, a driver's rather than a navigator's event was impressive. Andrew Russell and Jim won class awards on the Moorfoot three years in a row.

Border Motor Racing Club.
Jim drinks from trophy watched by (left) *Autosport* editor Gregor Grant
and (right) Andrew Russell.

New to single-seaters. Jim Clark at 25.

In 1958 Jim Clark's career gained a new car, a new team, and a new momentum, but as the programme for the new year took shape his mother began to worry about the dangers of motor racing. It was inevitable following the toll of years such as 1957 when Ken Wharton, Eugenio Castellotti, Herbert Mackay Fraser and Bill Whitehouse died. Alfonso de Cabeza Vaca, the 17th Marquis de Portago, died with his co-driver Ed Nelson and 10 spectators when he crashed on the Mille Miglia. The melancholy headlines continued in 1958 with six Formula 1 drivers dead from motor racing injuries and Mike Hawthorn, the new world champion killed in a road accident on the Guildford bypass in January 1959.

Jim's father was concerned about danger, but Jim's neglect of the farm was a pressing problem too. From a handful of weekends in 1957, half a dozen races and a few rallies, he was contemplating a programme of 17 race meetings not only in Scotland and the north of England, but abroad in 1958.

Quite apart from natural concern for Jim, there was the added worry about what would happen on the farm should he be injured. The family was only just recovering from the loss of his uncle and grandfather which had led to him leaving school.

Jim wanted his parents to come to terms with racing because he still regarded himself as inexperienced. At 23 he had far fewer racing miles under his belt than many of his rivals. Stirling Moss had been racing since he was 17.

Moss and Clark never raced on level terms. Moss was at the height of his powers as Jim was emerging and never regarded him as a rival, but then he never regarded any driver as a match for him. While Clark was haunted by self-doubt at the beginning of his career and deepening anxiety towards the end of it, Moss's jaunty self-confidence remained unabated until his crash at Goodwood on Easter Monday 1962. He liked Clark but, as Rob Walker testified, no other driver as a competitor ever entered his mind: "I suppose this is how it should be. Moss said, 'Well he's a jolly fine driver and a very nice chap', but as a competitor against himself he didn't consider anybody. I think he was right, I don't think there was a driver then that could have looked at him."

Clark was finding the lifestyle congenial. Racing was fun, his curiosity about cars had been aroused and he wanted to experience as many kinds of racing as possible. Life as a professional sportsman with all it entailed was still not on the cards, only a handful of drivers such as Moss

1958. Jim Clark set records almost as soon as he took the wheel of the D-type.
Here he tackles sharp right-hander at end of Charterhall's long straight.

Dawn of new decade.
Motor racing still simple, amateur, and fun.

were doing that, but the possibilities of earning a living at least a match for what he received from the farm were beginning to open up. He did not contemplate cutting himself off from the farm, which was why his farm steward or manager was so important and why he never looked ahead more than one year at a time.

His journeys to races also opened up other possibilities. Personable young men who raced Porsches were thin on the ground in 1957. Even club racing had its groupies and Jim discovered more girls than would crop up in the ordinary way on the farm.

Yet as parental pressure to curb his activities increased so did encouragement to continue from Scott Watson and Jock McBain. The Border Reivers wanted into sports car racing and looked round for a suitable vehicle. Its principal driver was to be Jimmy Somervail and, when he was unable to leave the farm, Jimmy Clark. The partners saw what they wanted in an Autosport advertisement. The Jaguar D-type, chassis number XKD 517, TKF 9, sold by Henlys in 1955 to Liverpool garage owner Gilbert Tyrer (who raced the famous 1940 Mille Miglia BMW) and Alex McMillan was up for sale.

In 1956 TKF 9 had passed to the Murkett Brothers, Jaguar dealers in Huntingdon, who painted it white for grand prix driver Henry Taylor, later Ford Motor Company's competitions manager, to drive. Taylor crashed it at Silverstone, scored a win at Snetterton, and a third at Spa-Francorchamps in 1957 before the car was sold to McBain, with a full-width windscreen to comply with sports car regulations. It had a head fairing, but as a production D-type lacked the shapely tail fin of the works competition cars.

Raced by Jim Clark it finished every one of its 20 events, 12 times in first place, before being disposed of in the winter of 1958-1959 to Alan Ensoll, and converted to a replica of an XKSS road car. It was then bought by Bob Duncan of Crumlin, raced in Northern Ireland before being restored by Shrewsbury solicitor Bryan Corser in 1964. He returned it to its proper shape, painted it British racing green, and lent it to me for a test alongside his XK120 and C-type at Oulton Park for a feature in *Autocar* magazine.

In 1979 TKF 9 was bought by Willie Tuckett of Devon who drove it in many historic events including, by a fine irony, the great 1990s tours of Scotland run by Scottish farmer John Foster under the collective title "Ecurie Ecosse."

Scott Watson changed the Porsche from silver to white, making it easier to see at dusk. He was serious about road safety.

Winners take all.
Jim Clark garlanded in victory shows strain of race.

FULL SUTTON TO SPA

Jim Clark's first D-type race on the airfield circuit at Full Sutton in Yorkshire earned him a place in the record books as the first driver to lap a British circuit at an average speed of over 100mph in a sports car. The contrast with bumpy disused Charterhall was profound. Full Sutton had a long 3.2 mile lap and was in perfect condition. The American Air Force had just spent a quarter of a million pounds – a lot of money in 1958 – resurfacing it.

It was characteristic of Clark that because the Reivers did not have a trailer and Edington's old farm lorry was out of service, he should drive the D-type with no heater and no hood straight to the circuit on a frosty night in early April. "I wrapped myself up in as many sweaters and coats as I could find, stepped into the D-type and set off through the slush of Berwick into a snow-storm and drove to York that night. I went through Newcastle at 11pm making a whale of a din."

Jim Clark did love showing off in a car.

He not only revelled in being in control of a fast car, he liked to prove that he was in control. Showing off in cars may have been part of his acquired extrovert nature, or it may even have been a symptom of the same shy disposition that preferred to hide behind a mask, or shroud itself in the confines of a car.

Some of his exploits on the road might be regarded as politically incorrect or anti-social in the 1990s even though they were no more than boyish fun in 1959. His relish at driving through Newcastle in the small hours with the D-type's open exhaust barking loudly was matched when he was driving its replacement, a Lister-Jaguar back to Scotland. He enjoyed a private race with a Ford Thunderbird, blasting past at 150mph. Clark estimated the Thunderbird was doing around 120mph and its driver's rear vision was obscured by a passenger. On a Sunday morning with the Lister's exhaust pipes on the left, it must been something of a shock to some luckless American Air Force officer.

Schoolboy fun? There were no open road speed limits in 1959.

The D-type represented a revival for the Border Reivers. The team was so loosely structured that it had almost come to pieces until promoting Jim Clark gave it a new purpose. Now, under its Galashiels reiver banner, it was

Wooly cardigan, JC driving gloves, Bell helmet, and Sally.

once again to be reckoned with. The 1958 season brought it 20 victories with Jim in the Jaguar and Porsche, and he also scored class wins in sprints and hill-climbs with his Triumph TR3.

He was proud of his unofficial record for the fastest time on the Rest-and-be-Thankful hill-climb in a TR3. It was a relatively obscure event on a disused road through Glen Croe in deepest Argyllshire but it fulfilled his desire to be the best with any car in any contest. Driving there from Duns brought him into contact with someone who would one day become his friend, keen rival, and confidant.

His route to the Royal Scottish Automobile Club's premier sporting event followed the north bank of the Clyde, one of the Firth's least picturesque stretches where it oozes between the Kilpatrick Hills and the flat lands of Abbotsinch. Hard by the oil storage tanks and subordinate docks of Bowling at the western terminus of the Forth and Clyde canal lies Milton, and in the 1950s the local Jaguar dealer was Stewart's of Dumbuck.

Jim Clark knew Jimmy Stewart for his polished driving of the Ecurie Ecosse Jaguars. In 1954 Stewart had been injured in a works Aston Martin at Le Mans and after crashing again the following year, doctors told him he could not risk another. He hung up his helmet. His mother had never liked him racing and, true to form, gentle, gallant, courteous Jimmy Stewart gave up. It was difficult for him later to accept his brother Jackie gaining the fame and fortune to which he had come so close.

When Jim Clark stopped off at Dumbuck in 1958, he was already a minor celebrity. Jackie Stewart was thrilled to meet him: "Even then he was somebody special. He had just lapped Full Sutton at 100mph in the D-type. He was somebody I knew I should be looking at. I ran from the house next to the garage, his TR3 was under the canopy getting filled with Esso Extra." Jim's sartorial style was a puzzle to Jackie even then. "Jimmy never changed very much. He was wearing a flat cap and a blue round-necked sweater with a collar and tie."

Clark had been apprehensive about driving the D-type. He claimed it was too fast for him but, after a test session at Charterhall where he frightened himself with its speed along the main straight, he agreed to race it. It had a beautiful engine, he said, and he thought the prospects for 1958 stimulating.

Scott Watson's strategy was to extend Clark's reach, and after handling the high speeds at Full Sutton, he entered both the D-Type and the Porsche for sports car races at Spa-Francorchamps in Belgium.

Spa was one of the fastest circuits in Europe. A triangle of public roads measuring 8.76 miles in a picturesque wooded valley of the Belgian Ardennes near the border with Germany. Well-surfaced, with sweeping bends, and blisteringly fast, it had one of the longest straights in motor racing, and a long curving climb back to a natural amphitheatre round the start and finish. The lap finished with a hairpin bend and a spectacular downhill rush past the pits.

A track of high drama ever since it opened in 1924, it staged a touring car 24 hours race which somehow never attained the lustre of Le Mans. The Belgian Grand Prix was dominated by the German teams in the 1930s and it was one of the first grands prix to be revived after the war, in 1947.

In the 1950s it was still public highway in the best road-racing tradition, still with its Masta Straight, slightly downhill for almost two miles, where cars reached close to 200mph before the war. Only the bravest and fastest drivers took the kink in the middle of Masta flat-out, and the track was chiefly remembered in Britain for the accident which claimed the life of Richard Seaman, one of the best English drivers of the 1930s, at the wheel of a factory Mercedes-Benz.

The D-type had been there before with Henry Taylor, but to Jim Clark, Spa was a new experience which he did not much like. The opposition included Masten Gregory, a driver he sincerely admired, in an Ecurie Ecosse Lister-Jaguar. There was Paul Frère (Aston Martin), Olivier Gendebien (Ferrari Testa Rossa), Carroll Shelby (Aston Martin), Jack Fairman (Ecurie Ecosse Jaguar D-type), Ivor Bueb (Jaguar D-type), and Archie Scott Brown (Lister-Jaguar).

It was a far cry from Charterhall the previous weekend where the D-Type's brakes had locked at the end of the straight. Heat fused the copper compound of the pads with the copper deposit on the brake discs, an inauspicious omen for his first big international race on a track he had never seen. He had heard that it was fast, and confessed that had he had any idea what it was like he would have stayed at home.

Once again Scott Watson goaded him into action, gave him confidence, and even embarrassed him by talking about going into Formula 1. Scott Watson's altruism by now probably was on the

Hill-climb, 1958. Clark stopped at Jackie Stewart's en route.

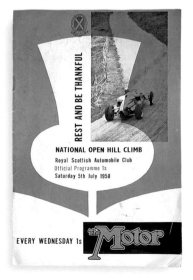

Rest-and-be-Thankful.
Clark takes hairpin in
Triumph TR3.
Military road of 1746,
A82 between Arrochar
and Cairndow.
Bypassed after 200 years
was adopted for hill-climb
course.

wane. He certainly regarded himself as Clark's manager. Clark regarded him as Clark's manager and cheerfully acknowledged that he would never have tackled such a programme of races without Scott Watson's constant nagging.

Once Scott Watson realised he was never going to be a driver he felt his role was to act as organiser, guru, administrator, and supporter, yet he still longed for responsibility on the organisational side of motor racing. Once he was made aware that his future did not lie with Jim Clark's affairs, he devoted himself to the BMRC and the Ingliston circuit near Edinburgh through its successor the Scottish Motor Racing Club (SMRC).

Meanwhile at Spa Jim Clark weighed up his urge to race, against doubts about his capacity to keep up with people whom he regarded as senior, like Masten Gregory. He agreed to race reluctantly at first, then became obliged to in order not to let the side down.

The Border Reivers shared a garage at Malmédy, scene of a second world war atrocity close by the Spa track, with Ecurie Ecosse. David Murray suggested that Jim should explore the circuit with an Ecosse driver, the experienced Jack Fairman, in a Volkswagen hire car. It was not unusual. Murray meant well. The idea was that Fairman would show Jim which way the corners went, where to brake, and where to accelerate. Jim preferred to find his own way round, but he went along with the suggestion.

Fairman not only showed him the famous course, but also the places where drivers and riders had died or been injured. There was a memorial where Richard Seaman crashed in 1939, and another at Stavelot where Bill Hollowell, the AJS rider died. By race day Clark was thoroughly unhappy, but recovered sufficiently to finish fifth in the 2.0 litre class with the Porsche in the morning GT event. It was wet and he had a close race with Wolfgang Seidel in an Alfa Romeo Giulietta, but when the rain stopped he lost the advantage, and the AC Bristols were able to overtake.

By the time the main event started at 4pm he was thoroughly nervous, and it was late in the race before he regained his composure. He was not sliding the D-Type in the way he described drifting the Sunbeam at Romannobridge. He was driving circumspectly and carefully, refusing to be drawn into contesting the lead with the big boys.

Clark was displaying a maturity and a coolness well beyond his racing experience. His programme for 1958 included racing on successive week-ends, but he was still new to the business and the caution he showed was to be a hallmark of his driving. He was able to hold speed in reserve throughout his career, rarely driving at what the late Denis Jenkinson, the veteran continental correspondent of *Motor Sport* would call "ten tenths", representing the top of a private scale "Jenks" invented to describe the effort required to achieve competitive speed.

Jim Clark rarely drove above "eight-tenths" and Spa could be described as a calibration exercise in which he would discover where the dividing lines lay. He was still in reality only driving at "six-tenths" of his potential, but it was the right way to proceed and many a novice would have over-reached himself and crashed.

Clark's performance at Spa exemplified the control which he could exercise in a racing car. It fulfilled the psychological proforma in which he could judge his driving with such pin-sharp accuracy that he hardly ever put a wheel wrong. But he was about to discover the penalties of a mistake.

It was a bitter experience. Masten Gregory and Archie Scott Brown shot ahead in their Lister-Jaguars. One of the handful of top racing drivers who wore glasses, Gregory, from Kansas City, inherited a fortune in 1951 and spent a good deal of it on racing cars. Impulsive to the point of recklessness he would not have been surprised to die in a racing car – indeed it would have come as no surprise to many of his rivals – yet he survived until a fatal heart attack in 1985 at the age of 55.

He lapped Jim Clark in a howl of noise and a rush of wind which shook TKF 9 as much as it surprised its driver. "Masten went steaming past well out in the lead with the Lister-Jaguar all sideways, his arms crossed up and fighting the steering. I felt a sudden twinge of shock and thought, 'To heck with this, if this is motor racing, I'm going to give up now.' I didn't think anyone could drive as quickly as that."

Professional initiative, studio portrait by Patrick Benjafield.

Two Ecurie Belge cars, an Aston Martin DBR2 driven by Paul Frère and a Ferrari Testa Rossa by Olivier Gendebien came past too and Clark thought he might try and slipstream them. He was almost as quick as they were until just before the kink in the middle of the straight, when he strayed out of their aerodynamic wake. The car was abruptly blown bodily across the track. It was doing about 175mph. He had never averaged over 100mph until about a month before and was thoroughly scared.

Worse was to come. Scott Brown was in something of a career crisis. At 31 he was growing reconciled to making little headway in Formula 1,

1959, the Border Reivers' Lister.
Jim treated it with respect after Scott Brown's accident.

his private life was in turmoil, his garage business not going well, and he had just been badly beaten by Gregory at Silverstone. Born with only one good hand and arm, he needed a special dispensation to race at all, and he too was having a difficult time with David Murray over joining Ecurie Ecosse.

The leading cars were so close that Scott Brown's car dented its nose on the tail of Gregory's Ecosse car on the third lap. One of Spa's notorious rain showers then moistened part of the track and Scott Brown, in the lead, crashed heavily. His Lister's wheel spinner scraped along the face of the memorial to Richard Seaman. The car fell on its side and caught fire, and despite the bravery of Belgian gendarmes who defied its exploding Elektron and magnesium components, the driver was fatally burned.

Billy Potts, the cousin with whom Jim drove in the 1955 Scottish Rally was at Spa with the Reivers' team when Archie Scott Brown died: "Jim was very quiet about it. He didn't say much, but you could tell he was distressed. The night of Scott Brown's crash we went along to the hospital, and he had been conscious and speaking, and the surgeon said, 'He'll die you know'. We said 'How – why?' But more than two-thirds of his body was covered in terrible burns. It was quite shattering to be told cold-bloodedly that he was going to die."

Scott Brown's accident was Clark's first close brush with death on a circuit. He came through the shower of rain, and caught sight of the plume of smoke from the other side of the circuit and felt sure that somebody had been caught out by the sudden change in conditions. When the Border Reivers got its own Lister later, he was apprehensive. It was a similar car to Scott Brown's. He thought it was too fast for him.

The accident affected him deeply. He had met Archie only the day before but in the small Scottish motor racing community knew him well from his astonishing driving at Charterhall and in races like the 1955 British Empire Trophy at Oulton Park. He had been as amazed as everyone else by his control over big powerful cars, despite his disability. Jim Clark had to start learning how to cope with tragedy, to assuage its effects, and there seems little doubt that he forced upon himself from that day a faculty for repressing his feelings.

It was probably his only way forward, for he was sensitive by nature and although the 1958 season, his busiest yet, would allay much of his self-doubt about his driving, in its place came a new appreciation of the dangers of motor racing.

He detested Spa yet when he entered grand prix racing he won there four times. It was as though it sparked his tension switch, compelling him to produce his greatest effort. In the 1963 Belgian Grand Prix, on a rain-soaked track, his car was jumping out of gear. He went through the Masta kink with one hand holding it in, and kept faith with Chapman by not telling anyone. Clark was not invariably cautious. He showed amazing courage under stress.

The 1964 race was really Dan Gurney's in his new Brabham-Climax. Clark, Hill, and McLaren battled for second place behind him until the closing stages when Gurney came into the pits, out of fuel. Graham Hill took the lead, only to run out of fuel. Bruce McLaren took the lead, only to run out of fuel. Jim Clark passed him on the finish line but the bemused race officials forgot to give him the chequered flag. He stopped out on the track to commiserate with Gurney unaware that he had won his second Belgian Grand Prix.

In 1965 it was wet again and he was notably solicitous towards Jackie Stewart on his first drive at Spa. Well aware of what his new friend was facing after his own distressing times there, they were running first and second. Clark was leading comfortably, and backed off to conserve his car. Stewart in the BRM caught up, until Clark could see its orange nosecone in his mirrors. He told Graham Gauld: "I could see this speck in my mirrors on the straight and I suddenly thought it's pouring with rain, it's Spa, it's an awful place. If Jackie can see me, he'll maybe think he can catch me." With typical gallantry he put in some quick laps to stretch the gap, worried that the less experienced Stewart might risk driving too fast in pursuit.

The evidence is there in Clark's times between laps 19 and 25, when he calmly cut 10 seconds every lap to race ahead of his chum. Courtliness in motor racing had not yet perished in 1965.

But in 1959 he still had no distinct view of racing as a career, and refused to regard himself as anything more than an amateur racer until the final Charterhall meeting of the year, in which David Murray had entered a D-type for Ron Flockhart and a Tojeiro Jaguar for Innes Ireland. The better equipped Ecosse cars had the latest Dunlop R5 tyres, the less favoured Reivers were on old R3s. Ecosse had 3.8-litre engines against Jim's 3.4-litre.

Flockhart was 35 in 1959. He began racing in an MG TC ten years earlier, graduated to an ERA in 1953 and won Le Mans twice in Ecosse Jaguars. He drove in Formula 1 with Maserati, BRM, Lotus and Cooper, finishing third at Monza in 1956 in a Connaught. He suffered burns in a BRM in the French Grand Prix of 1957 and was one of the leading drivers of the day when he died in 1962 attempting the Sydney to London record in a North American Mustang second world war fighter aircraft. Ireland was younger but was about to sign for Lotus in 1959 after impressing Colin Chapman with a stirring drive in the Rheims 12 Hour race.

It was the first time Clark drove the D-type to its limit, finding he could give both Ecosse cars a good run for their money. Ireland spun the Tojeiro and Jim was satisfied with finishing a close second to the experienced Flockhart. Clark's worry about over-reaching himself and being carried away by the excitement abated when he found he could keep up with both drivers without becoming over-wrought.

He still did not know much about racing cars or how they were supposed to handle. The D-type had plenty of power and taught him more than he would have learned in Formula Junior. He believed that a driver must know his limits and drive within them, although sooner or later he may have to overstep them or else never know what the limits were. His rule of thumb was to reassure himself after a corner that he could have gone through it quicker without going off the road.

Jim surprised himself by setting up identical winning times with his Triumph TR3 and the Porsche in the MG Car Club sprint at Stobs Camp near Hawick, where I became reacquainted with him. He also drove both at Rest-and-be-Thankful and won the Border Rally in the Triumph with his friend Andrew Russell.

He recalled fondly the rallies he did with Andrew Russell as among his happiest experiences at the wheel.

He would never enjoy such carefree driving again. Now he was analysing accidents. He was rationalising in the classic racing drivers' way when he saw another driver make a mistake, satisfying himself that he would not have done the same. It may have been illusory but it helped him come to terms with the reality of prolonged exposure to danger. Motor racing medical facilities were still primitive; Louis Stanley of BRM, apparently self-important yet crucially concerned about motor racing safety had yet to lead the revolution in providing proper emergency services.

The only flaw in Clark's comforting analysis was the knowledge that his fate could be wrenched from his own hands by a mechanical failure.

He finished a creditable eighth behind Fairman's Ecosse D-Type in that first race at Spa but the experience affected his attitude towards racing although perhaps not in the way he thought. He may have felt he was coping, but all the signs suggest that he was suppressing his real feelings in the struggle to control them. He was best able to regulate them when he

was at the wheel of a racing car. It became more than a sport, or a career, or even an obsession. It became an addiction.

Clark's emotions were like those experienced by wartime fighter pilots who had to close their minds to the frequent, sudden losses of comrades. They became cautious about relationships with fellow-pilots. They had to believe they were more skilful, more adroit or even just luckier than those killed. They had to find explanations for their survival to relieve their doubts and often suffered a sense of guilt when they came through unscathed.

The only way Jim Clark could prove to himself that he was more skilful or more adroit was to win. His means of applying the control he craved was to raise his level of stress which thus improved his powers of perception and reaction in accordance with the British Journal of Psychiatry findings I described. His powers of concentration must have been enormous, probably evidence of a keen intelligence and immense self-control. The cold baths at Loretto were having their effect.

It was from this self-control as much as natural ambition that his hunger for victories stemmed. Pressing forward his attack in the early stages of a race, the Clark hallmark of race tactics, was how he could best display control and ease the psychological longing that was now compelling him towards the next big step in his career, the Lister, Lotuses, and single-seater racing.

The D-Type served the Reivers well, and for 1959 Jock McBain was contemplating Formula 2. Clark looked ready for a single seater drive and a front-engined 'mini-Vanwall' Lotus seemed a likely prospect. In the autumn of 1958 McBain arranged for him to try one. A test session at Brands Hatch was set up although Jim had not only never driven a single seater racing car, he had never driven at Brands Hatch, the tight little circuit in Kent soon, in 1964, to hold its first British Grand Prix.

Driving there was a daunting experience, but proved the most important turning point yet, because he showed his potential within a very few laps. Skilled drivers do not require to work themselves up to a competitive lap time; if they have the ability they show it at once. It was the start of his fascination with the man who inspired and motivated him for the rest of his life, Anthony Colin Bruce Chapman.

Jim began the test in front of a distinguished audience. Cliff Allison, who had just signed for Ferrari, Graham Hill, Innes Ireland, Alan Stacey and Keith Greene were all either in Formula 1 or just about to enter it. As he drove off he failed to locate the brake pedal in the narrow cockpit and wondered what would they think if he wrote the car off on Paddock Bend. They would never believe he simply could not find how to stop the thing.

Once again his apprehension about looking foolish asserted itself. He need not have worried. He asserted his control, and Chapman was busy being impressed until Scott Watson revealed that not only was Clark new to single-seaters, but he was new to Brands Hatch as well. Chapman immediately called him in under the impression that he must be driving beyond his capacity. It was a common reaction to Clark's speed among people accustomed to ordinary mortals; it was simply unbelievable that anybody could be this good without over-reaching himself.

Chapman sent Clark out again in a Lotus Elite which Scott Watson was thinking of buying, his commercial impulses over-riding any fleeting concern he might have entertained about Jim spinning off the track. In any case he could see how smoothly and competently Clark was driving and had no qualms about releasing him for a second session in the Formula 2 car. Clark was lapping in 58.9sec, which goaded its regular driver Graham Hill into responding with 56.3sec, an unofficial lap record. Hill must have been startled to find a novice going so fast.

What happened next affected Jim acutely. He climbed out of the car, Graham Hill took it over, and a wheel fell off. Paddock Bend was a fast downhill right-hander after the pits, made difficult for drivers who could not see the apex from the approach, and had to aim for a point in space out of sight over the crest of the hill. The Lotus overturned, Hill was flung clear, and Clark was horrified. He resolved never to drive anything so fragile. The Elite was deemed satisfactory instead, and Scott Watson put it on his shopping list for 1959.

The car was to be ready for the Boxing Day Brands Hatch meeting. Clark and Scott Watson took the overnight train to London, picked it up at the Green Park Hotel and had time only to drive down the A20 to Brands Hatch, and tape up the headlights before practice.

Encountering Colin Chapman in a race in another Elite proved he was not only a brilliant engineer, but a formidable and competitive driver. It also proved that the new young and

Jim Clark explains Lotus Elite to Jimmy Scott of the *Edinburgh Evening News*.

Peter Arundell sympathises after Clark's engine fails
on first lap of disastrous 1966 Belgian Grand Prix.
Clark does not seem moved.

relatively inexperienced Jim Clark was more than a match for him. *Motor Sport* was sceptical, intimating that it was only because Clark's production Elite had all the latest modifications that he was able to stay ahead of Chapman until a back-marker got in the way. Once again there was sheer disbelief among the onlookers that this relatively unknown driver could surpass an acknowledged expert. Some other explanation for his speed had to be found; in this case "the latest modifications". It was a hypothesis Chapman cheerfully encouraged since it inferred that production Elites were as fast as the factory car. Clark's performance was simply incredible and at Brands he not only matched Chapman whose ability was well proven, but entirely outperformed his effective second-in-command, the experienced Mike Costin, who would also have a role to play in years to come.

If Jim Clark was enthralled by Chapman, Ian Scott Watson was less easily charmed. He knew the car Chapman was selling him to be less than factory fresh and prepared for trouble. Jim had grown up in a culture of trust in which you could safely buy beasts from Dublin unseen; you knew you would get your money's worth. Almost to the last he believed people were, by and large, as truthful as he was. No cynicism, no deceit, no cant.

Alas, such probity may not have been the best credential for a career in front-rank motor racing. Almost alone Scott Watson was cautious, alert to the pitfalls that lay in wait for the unwary but his counsel was about to be rejected. Any suspicions Jim may have had about the wide world outside Scotland were well founded even though they were not well articulated. What was certain was that his destiny was being shaped. It lay with Lotus and with Colin Chapman.

Walter Hayes: "There is no explanation of a God-given talent, because what happened at Brands was really like the second coming. It was an amazing thing. And it's really what blew Chapman's mind more than anything else. He would have killed really to have signed Clark, because he knew what he'd got. Jimmy was a great secret weapon for Chapman. For him it was like discovering diamonds at Kimberley."

Drivers making exits were regular feature. Serious consequences rare in club racing became frequent feature of professional racing.

1964, Goodwood International Trophy,
Jim Clark's 25th Formula 1 race victory.
He went on to win 24 more.

SINGLE SEATERS

In 1959 Jim Clark raced the Reivers' Elite against one belonging to Graham Warner, proprietor of The Chequered Flag, a sports car dealer. Warner had ambitions to move into Formula Junior, an apprentice class of single seater racing devised in Italy for cars based on components and engines from production road cars. It was soon to gain international recognition, and Chequered Flag was keen to build a car for it. The formula looked like being a success, attracting plenty of keen young amateur drivers, and Warner wanted to sell them racing cars for the track as well as sports cars for the road.

There were still relatively few racing car constructors in Britain, so the only way to do it was set up a small factory. Warner acquired a prototype, took on a development engineer, and called the result Gemini after his birth-sign. The front-engined car had a well-proportioned space-frame, independent suspension, and could be equipped with either a BMC A-series or Ford 105E engine. Either way a BMC gearbox was standard, with a transfer box to lower the drive-line.

It did not look strong, especially at the back where its fixed-length driveshafts and strut suspension had a spindly appearance, yet it worked well and exceeded Warner's expectations when 30 were made, mostly for export to the United States.

Those were pioneering days. The established manufacturers of Lola, Cooper, and Lotus were waiting to see if the formula would be a success. Jim Clark was expected to drive the Elite at the Boxing Day Brands Hatch meeting in 1959 and, after a season in which he had been able to watch Clark's competence from the close proximity of another Elite, Warner invited him to drive in the Formula Junior race as well. It was the Gemini's debut, and Clark's first race in a single seater.

The cockpit was close-fitting and the Speedwell-tuned Austin engine troublesome. By the time Clark reached the start he was cold and dispirited, and the battery was flat. He looked enviously at Alan Stacey alongside him on the starting grid in a sleek mid-engined car different from everything else. Hurriedly finished, not even painted, it was the first Lotus 18. And even if it was not handling well yet, it was about to set Lotus on the road to stardom. Clark got under way with a push but it was a discouraging

Brands Hatch, Formula
Junior October, 1960.
Tony Maggs (Gemini)
pole position on the
left of the front row
finished third,
Clark (Lotus 18 alongside
him) was second,
and the race was won by
Peter Arundell (Lotus 18
alongside Clark).

Clark's Aston Martin connections revived in the
DB4GT Zagato at Goodwood in the 1962 TT.

experience. His mood was not helped after a close encounter
with Graham Warner in the GT race. On the last lap, having
settled for second place Clark lost control of the Elite on the
wet track, hitting the bank and breaking a rear hub.

It was an unhappy way to finish his last race in one of
Scott Watson's cars and since it was also the first crash of his
racing career it shook his confidence. He never understood
why he lost control, blaming the loss of concentration that
followed settling for second place. He never "settled" for
second place again.

Clark "retired" from racing regularly, but was quickly
reinstated by Jock McBain and Scott Watson who kept
pressing him to continue: "I'd say to them: 'Och, no, we
won't do that,' and they would say: 'Och, yes we will!' They
both deserve a lot of the credit for my world championships. Without them
I would probably have been quite content with my farm at Chirnside.
Racing drivers need somebody to encourage them when they are taking
their first steps, and carry them through bad spells. All drivers have bad
spells and your confidence often needs restoring."

By the beginning of 1960 Clark's confidence was growing, at the
wheel at any rate. But he knew he had to reappraise his position on the
farm after an approach from Reg Parnell to join Aston Martin's new
Formula 1 team.

Parnell had been racing since 1935, made his mark after the war with
Maseratis and an ERA, and drove for the Alfa Romeo team in the first world
championship grand prix at Silverstone in 1950. By 1959 he had retired
from driving and was managing Aston Martin's entry into grand prix
racing.

He had been told by Jock McBain of the great new driving talent that
was revealing itself in Scotland. The Aston was an elegant front-engined six
cylinder 2.5-litre car, and although Jim refused Parnell's first offer of a test
drive, he realised he had reached a crossroads; he could either carry on
racing as an amateur, or start a professional commitment which could take
him into the top level of the sport, and his father was complaining about
the time and money that was spent on Jim's hobby with no return.

Parnell arranged a test session on a wintry day at Goodwood, and
there was frost on the former aerodrome, which looked exposed and
uninviting. Clark went out in an Aston Martin DBR2 sports car with a 4.2-
litre engine, similar to the 3.0-litre which brought Aston its Sports Car

World Championship. It was the most powerful car he had driven, and the track was icy, yet he was astonished at how well it handled. It had good traction and was blisteringly fast. After a few laps, he tried the big single seater. It was a strong contrast with the small and comparatively primitive Gemini. The Aston was a serious car with enormous potential, and as soon as he climbed into it he knew his world was about to change. "I stared out at those enormous exposed wheels and tyres, and thought, 'This is it'."

The handling was not unlike the Lister-Jaguar he had been racing for Border Reivers. The power was in a different league however, even though nothing like the 300bhp the contemporary Ferrari was claiming. He gained confidence, yet remained apprehensive about handling it in race traffic.

Clark went back to Goodwood for a further test session with a 3.0-litre DBR1 sports car and the 2.5-litre Formula 1 car, but this time there was an interloper. He now knew he was likely to have offers from both Lotus and Aston Martin, and after winning the Lotuseer Trophy, for his performance in his first year with a Lotus, told Mike Costin that he was going to be testing the Aston the following Monday at Goodwood.

Costin, Chapman's number two and the third member of the Elite trio at the Boxing Day Brands Hatch meeting of 1958, turned up with the Formula Junior car and Jim found the handling a revelation. Once again he had reached a turning point.

The contrast between the swift, small, exquisitely-balanced mid-engined Lotus and the big, now old-fashioned and rather clumsy Aston Martin was profound. Clark could scarcely believe that any car could hold the road so tenaciously. He could go through St Mary's, an off-camber left hander with a deep dip in the middle, faster than he believed possible: "The car seemed to be glued to the road." Clark drove round Goodwood in 1min 36sec, four seconds quicker than any Junior had gone before.

There was more to come. Chapman wanted Clark to try the Lotus Formula 1 car, which was much like the Lotus 18 Junior with a 2.5-litre Coventry-Climax engine instead. However Clark had given Parnell his word that he would be available for the Aston Martin team if it came to the starting grid, which was still in doubt. If the car had been available a year earlier it might still have stood a chance, but Parnell was offering him £600 a year to stand by to drive it.

Starting grid conference. Clark (in Lotus 18) consults Trevor Taylor (at front) and Mike Costin.

He accepted, but after driving the Lotus, astonisingly he went back to Parnell and said, "Colin

Ford publicity uses saloon car champion
John Whitmore on left, Jim Clark, and
Jackie Stewart.

Chapman has offered me a drive in the Lotus. He says he will pay more than you will. What do you think I should do?" He did not simply walk out on Parnell for the better offer. It was amazingly naïve yet entirely in character. Parnell to his credit said, "I think that following the changes to the regulations next year this car is probably not going to make it, and if you've got any sense you'll go to Lotus, so we will cancel our contract." Chapman took him on for Formula Junior and Formula 2 which was for 1½litre unsupercharged cars like the approaching Formula 1.

So even though he was still feeling his way in motor racing diplomacy, Clark was now a professional racing driver. He would meet Parnell at the Steering Wheel Club in Brick Street, Mayfair, which had a small dining area, and the regulars included many of London's used car dealers and drivers such as Stirling Moss, Mike Hawthorn, and Peter Collins. In the 1950s they did not get into private aircraft and fly to races. They drove, and when they came back made Thursday a big night with Moss sitting on the stairs telling everybody what had happened, and Hawthorn at the bar with his pints of beer.

In such company Clark seemed stand-offish, shy, and slightly suspicious. David Benson met him and Clark took him for one of Parnell's team, there to talk about his contract, displaying all his characteristic misgivings of strangers.

The Aston initiative collapsed half way into the season. It was the last year of the 2.5-litre formula, and a new 1.5-litre car was not planned. Clark was arriving at the end of an era of big cars, strict team managers, and team tactics. Team motor racing was on the way out, and driver motor racing on the way in. The world championship was in its tenth year and the focus was now firmly on the men at the wheel rather than the cars and manufacturers. From now on it would matter less who made a car than who drove it, so much so that before long the name of the car would be smothered by the name of the sponsor.

The Border Reivers' plan for 1960 was to sell its Lister-Jaguar and take on the Aston Martin DBR1 3.0-litre, rebuilt after the fire at Goodwood. Clark's programme then embraced sports cars, Formula Junior, and Formula 2. It was time to give racing a real try in 1960 and come to terms with at least a spell away from day to day management of the farm.

Bill Campbell was put in charge as farm steward. "I knew I could trust him implicitly to keep the farm rolling along without my constant

The Reivers' veteran Aston Martin DBR1 finished third at Le Mans in 1960
with Clark and Roy Salvadori.

Partnership forged, Jim Clark and Colin Chapman.

supervision." Confidence, trust, and keeping things in the family were still the principles by which Jim Clark ran his life. His commitments to Aston Martin and Lotus kept him from driving the Reivers Aston in some events, but it gained a creditable third place overall at Le Mans with Roy Salvadori co-driving. It was a tremendous achievement to split the Ferraris with a rather battered old Aston, and probably the last great amateur achievement of his career.

The 1960 season marked Jim Clark's graduation into the front ranks of motor racing and the front rank of driving. No more would *Motor Sport* seek to explain his performances by suggesting that his car was somehow superior. His succession of victories throughout the year with the Lotus 18 running in all three single-seater categories marked him out as a driver of distinction. There was no longer any doubt that he was a proficient committed sportsman for better or for worse.

The whole course of life now changed. He forsook the cosy world of club racing, the Border Reivers, and Ian Scott Watson, and entered the realms of professional grands prix. Ian had remained effectively his manager in his first year driving for Lotus. He made all Clark's travel arrangements, but in the end received a letter from a member of Jim's family, saying he was no longer required. He stepped back and took up other interests. He still went to grands prix from time to time, but things were never the same between them again.

The break-up hurt Ian deeply. Who was to blame? It was an uncharacteristic delinquency. Ian refused to fault Jim. It abrogated the great friendship that had flourished between them, and almost coincided with when Clark fell out with Innes Ireland as well. Somebody was evidently worried that there could have been a misunderstanding about the apparently intimate nature of Clark's and Scott Watson's relationship. On mature reflection Scott Watson could almost understand why; after all they shared rooms and looked inseparable, although anybody who knew either would have found the suggestion laughable.

Scott Watson regretted the sense of betrayal he felt, but found it difficult to broach the subject ever again with Jim Clark. He felt there was a new influence in Clark's life; it transcended motor racing although it was part of it. Jim seemed to have become mesmerised by Colin Chapman.

When regular driver John Surtees (left) dropped out for motorcycle race, Chapman put Clark in. Zandvoort 1960 was Formula 1 debut.

Tipo 156 Ferrari, von Trips at the wheel.

ITALIAN IMBROGLIO

The worst accident of Jim Clark's career took place at Monza, in the Italian Grand Prix of 1961. It was always believed that the chain of events that set it off was an ill-judged manoeuvre by the principal victim, Graf Berghe (Taffy) von Trips, driving into Clark's path. Jim Clark certainly believed as much, and suspected that having overtaken his Lotus, von Trips dismissed it as a competitor and did not believe it would ever catch up.

Yet Stirling Moss, who was behind the leading quartet of cars, thought differently. He was sure that the accident was set off by Ricardo Rodriguez who pushed across making for the corner, von Trips had nowhere to go, went outwards and collided with Clark. Rob Walker remembered: "I've never heard anybody else say it but I recall Stirling doing so within hours of it happening. He was in a position to see the whole thing."

Wolfgang von Trips, on the verge of the world championship.

The Rodriguez brothers were new to grand prix racing. They were rich, accustomed to success, but at best impetuous and at worst arrogant. Ricardo, the younger, was the more talented, possibly the more ambitious, and he was determined to make an impression. Champion Mexican motorcycle racer at the age of 14, he won his class in the 1957 Nassau Tourist Trophy at the wheel of a Porsche and in 1960 set off with brother Pedro to race a Ferrari for the North American Racing Team (NART). Success came quickly and seemingly easily, with second at Le Mans in a 250GT, third at Sebring, and second at the Nürburgring 1,000kms with Pedro.

In practice for the fatal race at Monza, Ricardo proved almost as fast as his team leader and world championship contender von Trips, but on the opening laps of the biggest race of his career, he was not aware of the fine points of etiquette still customary among top professional drivers in 1961.

Ferrari entered four cars, lending a fifth to Giancarlo Baghetti who had just scored a spectacular victory in his first grand prix at Rheims. The regular Ferrari drivers were Phil Hill, Count von Trips, and Richie Ginther in the latest Type 156 cars. Their Jano V-6 engines were modified by Carlo Chiti, who opened the 65 degree cylinder angle out to 120 degrees, making the car lower. Such a wide engine would never have fitted between the front wheels, so it was the first mid-engined Ferrari. Owing to their better balance the 120 degree engines revved to 10,000rpm instead of 9,500 rpm.

Rodriguez, as the newest member of the team, had the old 65 degree engine. The difference in power was slight, but it may have provided a further stimulus for him to prove that his driving was a match for anybody even with a sub-standard car.

The Italian Grand Prix was an end-of-season slipstreaming pursuit race with the teams at the top of their form. The Monza banking had been a controversial feature since its reconstruction in 1955, and the road portion of the circuit had three slow corners. Otherwise it was flat-out all the way and very fast. The bankings were full-bore in 1.5-litre cars, and the field passed the main grandstand twice per lap. The first time was coming off the south banking and racing off towards the fast Curva Grande, the second time accelerating out of the relatively slow Parabolica and into the north banking. The two streams of cars were separated, astonishingly, only by a row of traffic cones.

The banked circuit was used for the Italian Grands Prix of 1955 and 1956 but nobody liked it much, and when the entire Ferrari team was plagued by tyre and suspension trouble in 1956, the race reverted to the road circuit. The track promoters and the Automobile Club of Milan tried to revive the bankings in 1957 and 1958 running races for Indianapolis roadsters in a vain attempt to bring the racing of the new and old worlds together. It never worked despite the financial attractions.

For 1960 the banked track was revived but the British teams refused to race on it because they said it was dangerous. In their absence Ferrari used the grand prix as a testing session for 1.5-litre engines ready for the new formula due in 1961.

The Automobile Club of Milan held its ground when the British teams protested against the reintroduction of the banked track in 1961, but with the new formula now established they agreed to come back anyway, and to allay their worries about safety, the length of the grand prix was reduced from 500 to 430kms. There was a robust response with 37 entries, including works teams from Ferrari, Cooper, Lotus, BRM, Porsche, and Tomaso, together with most private teams which were able to field a competitive 1.5-litre car.

The 1.5-litre formula had been introduced in an attempt to curb the power and speed of grand prix cars, so the 1961 cars were some 8sec a lap slower at Rheims, but within two years there was very little in it – around 2sec a lap – and at Monza the slipstreaming was as fast and furious as ever.

Rodriguez created a stir by occupying the first row of the grid alongside von Trips. Even his colleagues were reluctant to believe the timekeepers who claimed a 2min 46.4sec lap for him in the old 65 degree training car against von Trips's time of 2min 46.3 in the newer 120 degree car. Team Lotus had not yet any of the novel Coventry-Climax V-8 engines which Cooper, fresh from two world titles, was trying out. Rob Walker also had one in Moss's Lotus. Graham Hill tried a new BRM V-8 engine in practice but, like his team-mate Tony Brooks, made-do with a Climax four-cylinder like those in Clark's and Ireland's Team Lotus cars.

The starting grid, unusually for the time, was arranged in staggered rows of two cars each instead of the customary 3-2-3 or even 4-3-4. The organisers knew the Ferraris would be fastest and were trying to let the red cars get clean away from would-be slipstreamers. Accordingly the 32 starters presented Lord Howe who dropped the flag, with one of the longest starting grids yet seen in a grand prix.

The leading cars set off, with Clark, perhaps unwisely but understandably, up among the four Ferraris which made a slow-ish start on account of pulling very high axle ratios, seeming to hang fire for a while before they really got under way. "They were all in such a tight bunch and jostling for position so continuously that a large tarpaulin would have covered the leading seven cars," according to *Motor Sport*. They were von Trips (Ferrari 120), Rodriguez (Ferrari 65), Richie Ginther and Phil Hill (Ferrari 120s) who made up the second row, Giancarlo Baghetti (Ferrari 120) from row 3, Clark from row 4, and Brabham (Cooper-Climax) from row 5. Bonnier (Porsche) who shared row 4 with Clark, and Gurney (Porsche), Stirling Moss (Lotus-Climax) and John Surtees (Cooper-Climax) led the next group.

Graham Hill (BRM-Climax) who was on row 3 with Baghetti kept up briefly but fell back. An Yves Debraine photograph shows seven cars bunched on the banking just before the accident on the second lap. Phil Hill was in the lead closely followed by Ginther, then Clark lower down the banking, Rodriguez higher up, and Brabham in Clark's wake with von Trips and Baghetti bringing up the rear.

The stage looked set for a sweeping Ferrari victory. They had won four out of the season's six grands prix, only Moss's Lotus breaking them up in epic drives at Monaco and the Nürburgring. The Ferraris were ahead of the British in 1.5-litre engine technology, they were well-organised, and had

copious reserves of driver talent. Ferrari had embraced mid-engines, disc brakes, and was at the height of its powers.

Clark recalled a touch of the Roman Circus about the atmosphere. Everyone had come to see the Ferraris dominate the opposition. The British teams with their four-cylinder Climax engines, scarcely seemed to have a chance. He decided to slipstream the Ferraris.

"My plan of campaign was to get away as quickly as I could and move out in front. Then, when the first Ferrari passed me, I would slipstream as hard as I could and try to keep up. I managed to get a good start, but the pack was soon on my heels, and first Richie, then Phil, Jack and Ricardo all went past between the first and second laps. My engine was going really well, and though Taffy passed me on the Lesmo curves I managed to keep up with him right round the back, down the dip under the banked portion of the circuit, and round the Vialone curve which is flat out. I was still on his tail slipstreaming round the Vialone to keep up as we came down at full speed to the braking point for the North Curve. By this time I was preparing to overtake him, and my front wheel was almost level with his back wheel as he started to brake. Suddenly he began to pull over towards me and he ran right into the side of me. There was no other car involved."

This account is now in contention.

"I honestly think that Taffy never realised that I was up with him. I am sure that when he passed me he had decided that as he was in a faster car, I would be left behind. Everything happened at lightning speed. We touched wheels, and oddly enough I had a split second to think about the accident before it actually happened. I thought: 'God, he can't do this.' I remember mentally trying to shout at him to look in his mirror and see me. I had the brakes on hard by now and I just couldn't do anything, for he was braking hard too. My wheels started to lock and I left black marks, but I was too close to the edge of the circuit, and I could not go on to the grass because we were doing between 140 and 150mph. At that speed you just can't go on the grass. As he came across I couldn't get out of the way. There was a tremendous blur, and the Lotus began to spin round and round along the grass, coming to rest at the side of the circuit. Taffy's car shot off the road and into a fence which the crowd were leaning on before bouncing back on to the circuit, leaving the driver lying on the grass."

Clark recalled jumping out of the car, running over with a marshal and trying to drag Taffy's car back off the track. It was an automatic reaction, but even then he realised there was nothing to be done for von Trips. "I didn't really want to go over to where he lay."

Why did von Trips pull in front of Clark? He was an outstandingly astute driver, he had led more laps of the season's races than anyone, won two and finished second only to Moss at the Nürburgring. Two weeks earlier he had described Jim Clark as the fairest competitor in grand prix motor racing.

It seems almost incredible that he would not have noticed Clark's car in his mirrors. It now appears more than likely that the impulsive Rodriguez may have moved over while lining up and braking for the Parabolica. It may even have been involuntary, but it set off a chain of events which led to von Trips's car spinning and climbing the grass bank. It was motor racing's worst accident since the Le Mans disaster of 1955 and its repercussions went on for years. Its immediate result was to increase Jim Clark's dark depression and lead him to worry sincerely about his future in motor racing.

Phil Hill went on to win the grand prix and become world champion. Von Trips had been the best German driver since the war and remained so until the German-Austrian Jochen Rindt who ironically died on the same corner at Monza in a Lotus in 1970 to become the sport's first posthumous world champion.

Von Trips was popular, handsome, aristocratic, and skilled in sports cars as well as single-seaters. He had been European hill-climb champion in 1958, won the Targa Florio with Olivier Gendebien and drove brilliantly in the 1959 Goodwood TT in a small capacity Porsche, finishing second ahead of Tony Brooks in a Ferrari.

Baghetti drove Ferraris in 1962, defected to ATS, but was never again in the running for a repetition of his Rheims triumph, and died of cancer at the age of 60. Ricardo Rodriguez's career was tragically brief. He drove for Ferrari in 1962, but died in practice for the Mexican Grand Prix in a Lotus.

Jochen Rindt, the next German world champion wins at Zandvoort and hears of death of his friend Piers Courage.

The shadow of Monza hung over the rest of Jim Clark's life. When he won the world championship in 1963 he was still being pursued by the Italian police and the press, both looking for a new angle, or new information and more detail which, with the best will in the world, Clark could no longer supply. He remained sensitive about it and seldom spoke about it. "I have never willingly discussed this affair in public for two very good reasons, firstly because it is a very sad and painful memory, and secondly because it occurred with such tremendous speed that my recollections are limited."

Race marshal restrains Clark from assaulting Brian Naylor
after 1960 Oulton Park accident.

He never even discussed it in private. Jabby Crombac: "I was not at Monza when the accident happened and I did not see Jimmy until the beginning of the following season. It was something I never discussed with him. It was part of my routine of not bothering him. He never wanted to discuss it. I never talked about it with him. If he went off the road he would tell you what happened. But an accident in which people had been killed, was something you did not talk about."

David Benson recalled: "He never discussed the Von Trips accident with me. It was always difficult to talk to racing drivers about death, or a big accident where somebody was killed. I never discussed the possibilities of death with Jimmy. I did with Jackie later, but he had a more realistic attitude to it."

Clark was getting presentiments of disaster. Monza was preceded by what he regarded as an peculiar run of similar accidents. At the Oulton Park Gold Cup race of September 1960 he was engaged in a race-long pursuit of Innes Ireland in another F1 Lotus. Just before Lodge Corner, Brian Naylor in a JBW-Maserati slowed to let Ireland past, unaware that Clark was immediately behind. He pulled back across the track and Clark had no chance of avoiding him. His car climbed a banking, almost rolled, and he lost the chance of setting fastest lap in the second half of the race as he had in the first. His first fastest lap was worth £50, his second would have added £100 to his day's earnings and a marshal had to restrain him from forcibly making Naylor pay.

1964 Gold Cup: Clark 2nd in F2 race, wins saloon race in Ford Lotus Cortina.

Jim had agreed to stay overnight after the race. Scott Watson felt that he needed a rest following the accident. Suddenly, at 10pm, he said, "Now I'm going home." Scott Watson remonstrated, "The room's booked, you've had an accident. Drive back in the morning." But Clark would not hear of it and went off. Scott Watson was summoned at three o'clock in the morning by the Lancaster police to come and collect his friend who had apparently been unable to make up his mind which way to go at a Y-junction, and driven straight ahead, demolishing a sign, and wrecking the front of the Porsche. Indecision, delayed shock, or tiredness? We may never know.

In 1996 Chris Rea made a film about the incident, and in his researches unearthed a film that von Trips had shot from an on-board camera round Monza in 1960. It showed graphically three-quarters of a lap of the track, the film running out dramatically at the very spot where the crash occurred.

Lotus 25 was close-fitting.
Dark look from Clark, Chapman wonders where to put
foam padding.

Lotus, Formula I and Colin Chapman

When Jim Clark returned home between races he could still relax. It was a peaceful haven where he could take stock. Friends who remembered him from the carefree days of Charterhall and the Border Rally found him distracted. Getting back to Edington Mains was his way of letting himself unwind. He generally reverted to his old self after a few days among the locals, but invariably the phone would ring and Chapman would instruct him to get back to Silverstone for testing, or he would have to leave again for another practice, another race.

He still did not comprehend that he was famous. Indeed because there was little media pressure at that time he did not have external constraints to deal with. He did not handle the media well, but then he seldom needed to. When he did get into media trouble it was because they asked him to define things that he did not want to think about. In the early days they were always asking him, "Are you frightened?" He hated that question, and he would get tetchy if people asked it.

Most formidable engineer-driver combination in modern motor racing. Chapman, Clark, 1960.

Walter Hayes: "He had two centres in his life. There was Chapman. Not Lotus, – Chapman. And there was home in Scotland. He felt secure at home in Scotland, but he never quite felt secure with Colin, because when you would say to him 'Well Jimmy if there's something worrying you why don't you sit down and ask Colin'. He'd say, 'Well you know, it's very difficult'. He admired Chapman. He was very friendly with him, and had huge respect for him. In a way he loved him, but there was often a sort of nervous tension between them."

By 1961 Chapman's influence was overwhelming. The relationship was more than just that between a team manager and a world champion driver. He was essentially Chapman's world championship driver. It became a close personal relationship in which they clearly enjoyed each other's company and, while drivers of other teams went out on their own in the evening after a race or a practice session, Jim would almost always have dinner with Chapman.

They went everywhere together. Jabby Crombac was one of the small

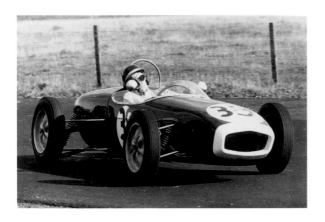

Charterhall, 1960. Lotus 18 Formula Junior.
Adaptable racing car with different engines.

close-knit Lotus family that shared hotel rooms because there was not much money to spare in motor racing in the early 1960s.

Crombac, small, articulate, multi-lingual had been a keen reader of *The Motor* and *Motor Sport*, and was a motor racing enthusiast to his fingertips. He went to Silverstone in 1948 and met Gregor Grant, then sports editor of *The Light Car*. The friendship blossomed when Jabby was taken on as a trainee racing mechanic by the celebrated French driver Raymond Sommer. Although never allowed to lay a spanner on an engine, he could touch bodywork and clean cars, and in the course of his work discovered a talent for gossip. As a source of information on the French racing world he was invaluable, and Grant printed it all as news.

Jabby was known as "the spy Hercules", and his material was so good that when Gregor started the weekly *Autosport*, to which the young Loretto schoolboy so looked forward every week, he appointed Crombac continental correspondent.

Jabby bought Colin Chapman's Lotus Mark Six and raced it so successfully in 1953 that *The Motor* called it, to Jabby's delight, 'preposterously fast'. It was. Chapman was quite relieved to see it go abroad because it had features, all perfectly legal of course, which he preferred to keep out of rivals' sight. Buying the car was enough to make Crombac Lotus's man in France, and a lifelong friend. His credentials included a long-standing friendship with Ron Flockhart which made him, in Clark's eyes, something of an honorary Scotsman.

Jim often shared a room with his colleague on the Lotus team, Trevor Taylor. Crombac would have a spare bed in the room so that the bill could be divided among three instead of two. When the team went to Indianapolis there were four in the same room, Chapman, Clark, Cyril Aubrey the timekeeper, and Crombac on the floor in a blanket.

Crombac's dedication to Chapman and everything to do with Lotus was a symptom of the intense loyalty Chapman could command. His leadership qualities transcended the creation of great racing cars, his enthusiasm was infectious, he clearly was brilliant, but more than that he had a gift for persuasion. He put his ideas over convincingly. He was able to sell his philosophy his sense of style and his self-confidence on both sides of the racing world and when it came to it, on both sides of the Atlantic. There was a messianic quality about him.

When he reflected on his achievements, Chapman could say quite un-self-consciously: "A few of us have to achieve great things in life so that it gives hope to others who are striving to achieve." He really believed that some people, like himself, had to succeed extravagantly in order to light up the lives of others. If anyone else had said anything of the sort it would have sounded arrogant. Chapman could say it so reassuringly that it seemed almost modest and quite self-evident. He had the natural vanity of a man who knew his ideas were better.

Walter Hayes was one of Chapman's most loyal and vigorous supporters: "He never was arrogant. He merely knew better than anybody else. He also knew more."

Hayes as an editor, had taken Chapman on as a newspaper motoring correspondent: "I'd been told to reform the *Sunday Despatch* and cars were beginning to be the big thing. There was no popular ownership of cars in this country until 1955. Nobody owned a car unless they were a doctor or a lawyer or rich. There were governments after the war telling us that we shouldn't have cars at all. Sir Stafford Cripps wanted to tax them pretty well out of existence."

"I was looking for somebody who could encapsulate what I felt was going to be the age of the car, so I got hold of Colin Chapman who was beginning to be talked about. Chapman was willing to come along, because £5,000 a year was quite important to him. He was difficult because he loved road testing cars, but it was not easy to get copy from him on time."

Hayes was sensible to Chapman's design flair. "He was not a particularly good engineer, he would sit in a restaurant with a paper napkin and he would draw a car, and when he got to the engine he would just draw a box and write 'engine' on it. I don't think he knew much about engines. His mind was a ferment of ideas yet instead of saying we've got it now, let's perfect it, he always assumed that there had to be something added for next year. If you look at all the

Colin Chapman and Walter Hayes (right). Ford master-mind Hayes loyal champion of Chapman wisdom.

20 July 1963. Copybook performance.
Clark held off Dan Gurney (Brabham) to win British Grand Prix.
Delicate touch of opposite lock at Stowe Corner.

things he initiated in motor racing, more than any other man of our day, you often find he never stayed with anything quite long enough."

He compared Chapman with a later entrepreneur in a similar mould, the notable Scottish racing driver Tom Walkinshaw who created an immensely successful business building and racing cars. "Walkinshaw did everything he said he would do for me on the day and at the price better than I could have expected. The same went for Chapman, and I hear stories about him in which he is not a recognisable man to me. I know people are sometimes different with me. People are particularly nice when you hold the purse strings but I went and got Chapman because I knew him and I trusted him."

Lotus began with this son of the landlord at the Railway Hotel, Hornsey, building a car with Austin Seven parts for a curiously English form of motor sport. Trials involved seeing how far a lightweight and rather spidery car could climb a muddy hill. It was an engineering as well as a sporting challenge to which he rose magnificently. His trials cars were home-built, improvised and primitive masterpieces. His Austin was followed by a Ford-powered version, then a 750cc special for racing. He applied the same bent for engineering to his trials car that he later applied to Jim Clark's grand prix racing cars, a talent for innovation that blossomed into something approaching genius.

If Chapman had not been one of the most innovative automotive engineers of his generation he would have been a success at something else. He was single-minded and obsessional at whatever he turned his hand to. He was an accomplished racing driver, he designed boats and flew aeroplanes, showing aptitude at all of them. His competitive spirit was acute. Chapman never accepted the old aphorism about what mattered was taking part not winning.

He could never understand how anyone could want to do anything without winning, and his winning was done with style. He had a flair for appearance, a neat turn of phrase, and a gift for branding the Lotus identity firmly on all he did. His achievements were immense, and he made exciting, innovative – although sometimes exasperating – road cars.

A millionaire by his 40th birthday, he won five drivers' and six constructors' world championships, and was at the head of a £10,000,000 business and the controls of his own Piper Seneca two years before his 50th. He had charm; he could show patience, but anybody doing business with him needed to be important to merit much of either. He put in long hours at the factory, ran the racing team at weekends, and seldom stopped

Dutch artist Jan Apetz penned napkin apology after Jim Clark's brush with heavy-handed law. Zandvoort police chief duly signed.

to wonder why others did not do much the same. Energy, drive, talent and success were his hallmarks.

So was his short fuse, which sometimes went off in public such as with an overzealous policeman at Zandvoort. Clark and he both had well-documented punch-ups with Dutch policemen, Clark in 1963 Chapman two years later, accused of not having valid race passes. Clark got an apology, Chapman a bruised elbow.

Chapman's credentials as a driver included a close race in 1956 with Mike Hawthorn at the Whit Monday meeting at Goodwood. Both were in Lotus 11s, and Chapman won. After the memorable drive against Jim Clark at Boxing Day Brands in 1958 he claimed he could not associate the novice who had tried out cars at Brands Hatch with the mature and skilful driver who now raced against him. He and Mike Costin had tossed a coin to decide which would win.

It was virtually Chapman's last race. He was married and had a family and his involvement with the business made him much too valuable to risk in amateur racing. Getting Jim Clark to drive on a casual basis was better than having any other racing driver on a permanent basis.

His other gifts included an ability to read a rule book, decide what its compilers meant and then find a way to defeat them. He also had a powerful commercial instinct. Where other enthusiasts might have been content to dismantle, or cannibalise their first car to work on their second, Chapman sold it.

Lotus Engineering grew on the premise that people would build their cars from kits, and went into business on January 1, 1952, in north London. Chapman made the firm his full time job in 1955, married Hazel Williams who had provided the initial capital of £25, and employed Mike Costin as his chief assistant.

Chapman developed aerodynamic sports-racing cars, and hired out his talent as a designer to Vanwall and BRM. His self-confidence seemed justified when Lotus survived its first financial crisis, and a Lotus Formula 2 car with a Coventry-Climax engine was shown at the London Motor Show. The Elite road car appeared in 1957, a ground-breaking design in glass reinforced plastic of which nearly a thousand were made.

Lotus moved to Cheshunt in north London, and developed the Lotus 18, a multi-purpose mid-engined single-seater used for everything from

Formula Junior to Formula 1. It set the seal on Lotus's success when Stirling Moss won the 1960 Monaco Grand Prix. The Jim Clark partnership was still to come, and so were Chapman's brilliant innovations such as the monocoque bath-tub of the Lotus 25, rising rate suspension, inboard brakes, side radiators, and employing the engine as a stressed part of the Type 49. He demonstrated his radical approach to design when he reduced frontal area of a racing car by getting the driver to lie down, recumbent in a sort of hammock. Soon every other designer was following his lead.

Chapman's delight at outwitting the racing authorities over badly-framed regulations was only matched by the cavalier attitude he adopted towards customers. He was always careful never to become personally involved, but the sharp practice manners of Lotus in its kit-car and early Elite period enraged buyers. Their dilemma was that no other car had the same appeal. No other car had the Elite's combination of speed and roadholding together with purity of line and sheer raciness. Chapman held the technological aces.

He brimmed over with expertise and bright ideas, and he could be solicitous when it suited him. When Scott Watson drove the first Elite back from Brands Hatch, a conrod broke a mile from home. With little of Jim's reticence where money was concerned, he telephoned Chapman right away. He had just walked home leaving his £1,300 (£1,951 with purchase tax) car a smoking ruin, and was not best pleased when Chapman told him off for racing the car when it was still new. Scott Watson retorted that it was nothing of the sort. Lotus had made only one white car and it had been racing round Brands Hatch for weeks, on behalf of BBC Television. Chapman gave way at once and promised a new engine at Berwick station the following day; it was there, even though it was between Christmas and New Year.

Much the same happened later with Scott Watson's Elan. It had one of the first 1500 engines and threw a rod. Lotus never got round to replacing it, but when Scott Watson phoned Chapman, once again there was a new engine at Berwick next day.

Chapman was just as attentive over Jabby Crombac who was often owed money for Renault gearboxes for the Lotus 18. He was buying five-speed conversions and sending them to England. Chapman always paid on time.

Chapman charm.
Made you feel most important person he ever consulted then erased you instantly from his mind.

Lotus 30, 1964. Model for Can-Am cars yet never a success.
Ian Walker team car, 4.7 litre Ford V-8, 350bhp, finishing second at Aintree supporting race.

Crombac received special treatment as a member of the Lotus family and so also, Crombac thought, did Jim, convinced Colin would treat him generously. He felt sure they would never have clashed over pay because Colin needed him so much. It was a pious hope.

Jim was a poor negotiator. There was one occasion when he phoned Walter Hayes and said "I've got to meet you, it's very important." They met in London and talked around every sort of subject, then he said "Well what I really wanted to ask you is do you think Colin's paying me enough?' Hayes found it curious that he didn't know, because drivers ask each other and they talk to each other. Everybody in Formula 1 knew to the last cent what people were being paid. Hayes suspected that it never occurred to him from the beginning that there was money in motor racing.

Clark's technique for communicating with Chapman about cars was simpler. "I tell him what is wanted with the car and he works out how to do it. I'm rarely at the factory. The best time to do things is at races when everything's fresh in your mind. We make up a job list with thoughts of what to do, and the team tries to fix it."

Now with V-8 power, Clark communicated with engineers on winning formula.

Yet by comparison with the suave, urbane Chapman, Clark was something of a country boy when he joined Lotus. There seems little doubt that Chapman set about impressing him to ensure the smooth working relationship that lasted throughout their association. He was confident that Jim would sign up for the following year so long as the cars were successful and so long as his affinity with Chapman remained. It hardly faltered. Clark remained loyal even when asked what it was like to drive the thoroughly unsatisfactory Lotus 30 sports car.

Urged to make its shortcomings public lest its dismal performance reflected on his driving Clark refused. Public displays of pique were unforgiveable. It would have been disloyal to Chapman to disclose that it was anything less than agreeable. "It was a nice and forgiving car to drive. Other Lotuses take a lot more driving to get the best out of them," he said guardedly.

His loyalty was never in doubt although in private there were some ups and downs, and occasions when he told Chapman he would not drive a car until they had put it right. Rob Walker witnessed an incident between

August, 1965.
German Grand Prix,
Nürburgring.
Bernard Cahier's camera at
first corner for Clark
(Lotus No 1) outrunning
challengers. Jackie Stewart
(BRM), alongside him on the
grid already behind.
Graham Hill (BRM No 9)
nose-down under braking.
On left Dan Gurney
(Brabham No 5),
Mike Spence (Lotus behind
Clark and Stewart) and
Lorenzo Bandini
(Ferrari behind Hill).
Masten Gregory was 8th in
his last-but-one grand prix,
a whole lap behind.

Jochen Rindt and Chapman which showed the pattern such events followed.

Rindt was driving the first Lotus 72 with inboard brakes at Jarama, Spain, when the brakes failed at the end of the straight. The heat insulation had apparently failed at the inboard end of the front brake shaft and the bolts had sheared. He was doing something like 190mph and the car stopped inches from a barrier. Rindt was furious, shouting at Chapman, "I'm never going to drive that buggering car ever again in my life." The Walker team was in the next pit and overheard everything. Graham Hill was driving for Walker, having come straight from Lotus. "What happens next?" Walker enquired. Hill said, "There'll be a cooling off period of 15 minutes and then Chapman will get him in the corner and talk to him, and next thing you know he'll be driving the car again."

It happened exactly like that. Chapman's crisis management always worked. He was able to talk people round, although he was clearly tougher with drivers after Clark. Like many people exposed to motor racing bereavements he remained more distant to drivers afterwards. Jochen Rindt told Rob Walker: "I'm so keen to win the world championship that I'm even going to drive for Lotus." How ironical that a brake shaft fracture was involved in Rindt's fatal accident at Monza just as he clinched the 1970 world championship.

The most likely explanation of Clark's growing apprehension must include his awareness of the odds against him narrowing as he accumulated racing miles. While everyone, like Maurice Phillippe that incredible day at Snetterton, marvelled at his near-miraculous skill, Jim knew his limitations. He had seen too many accidents following either component failure or mischance and he was concerned enough about the risk of injury that once he had driven the Lotus 25 with its strong bathtub monocoque, he disliked racing a car with a tubular space-frame. Stirling Moss's Goodwood injuries were exacerbated by the collapse of his Lotus 21-based car's tubular structure.

Clark's famous Elite race at Brands Hatch against Chapman was decided by a spinning novice in an Austin-Healey Sprite. He was always concerned about becoming involved in somebody else's accident.

Jim Clark, Lotus 24, Aintree 200 1962. Sixth Formula 1 race win.

Hill (BRM) and Gurney (Brabham) pursue Clark in German Grand Prix, finished in that order.
Michael Turner's painting shows Clark's sixth victory in six grand prix races Lotus entered 1965.

First victory for 1½ litre Coventry-Climax V-8. Snetterton, April 14 1962, Lombank Trophy.
Michael Cooper shot of Stirling Moss (UDT-Laystall Lotus 24 No 7 soon to end his
professional career), Jim Clark (Lotus 24 No 3) Graham Hill (BRM No 9) and
John Surtees (Bowmaker-Yeoman Lola).
Moss led from pole but delayed with broken throttle. Clark won.

Fresh from his rural background, Jim Clark was just as susceptible to Chapman's blandishments as Jochen Rindt. Yet there was a difference Clark enjoyed over Rindt, Fittipaldi, Ireland, or any of the other Team Lotus drivers down the years. Rob Walker said: "I would think Jim was probably the only driver that Chapman was ever really fond of. I never saw them have a row."

By 1967 Clark was no longer the aggressive lead-at-any cost driver he had been. His approach was more measured, and although the dramatic Italian Grand Prix of 1967 was still to come, he worried about the car breaking under him. The nagging uneasiness about safety which he found such difficulty in articulating to most people could sometimes reveal itself in unguarded interviews.

For most of his career he had such faith in Chapman that he may not have believed Lotus cars were fragile. Innes Ireland had no such conviction, cataloguing Lotus failures in detail and at length, from hub bearings breaking up to rear suspensions falling off. Chapman, it seems, was able to talk Clark out of the idea that racing cars were brittle things, besides the problem may not have appeared so serious in the beginning. It was at its height when Stirling Moss and Michael Taylor crashed in practice for the Belgian Grand Prix at Spa in 1960. Moss's accident was due to the breakage of the left rear suspension on which some technical analysts had cast doubt, because Chapman had put such emphasis on saving weight that he had hit upon a novel design in which the wheel was mounted on a light alloy hub carrier with a bottom wishbone and trailing radius arms. The suspension medium was a combined coil spring and damper unit, and the drive-shaft acted as the top wishbone. It was an imaginative concept, but its flaw was that if the drive-shaft broke, the wheel came off.

Moss crashed heavily at Burnenville, a long curve taken at about 130mph. The wheel parted company with its attachments at a bump on the exit from the corner, the car hit the bank, throwing the driver out where he suffered a broken nose and back injuries. They were not serious, but as with Jim Clark's accident at Hockenheim years later, the fact that Stirling Moss had had an accident was sufficient to cause serious loss of confidence in the paddock. Drivers who had persuaded

Leading 1962 French Grand Prix, Clark discovered loose bolt in front suspension. Car steered straight on corners. Julius Weitmann caught pain.

Spa, fourth successive
win, 1965.
Graham Hill quicker
in practice but Clark led
from lap 1.

themselves that they were clever enough to outwit danger felt vulnerable. The "control factor" they held dear no longer held good. If a driver was not in total control, the whole psychological function of motor racing was lost.

When Moss crashed the grandstands fell quiet. The paddock fell quiet. Spectators, teams, officials, and above all drivers struggled to come to terms with how motor racing could still harbour the unexpected and cut down the best driver in the world. It was a moment when it was shown up as a precarious business.

Moss, like Nelson at Trafalgar, had been cut down by what everybody agreed was a long shot. But it brought home the risks when he fell victim to an unlucky chance, a risk he always knew was present. If it happened to Moss it looked as though the risk was higher than anybody thought. As soon as the nature of the accident became known even the most confident, brash, and self-assured driver took stock. All that stood between a driver and disaster was an engineer trying to build a racing car as light and as competitive as possible. Drivers were prepared to take risks; it was part of the excitement. So long as they thought they were in control of 95% of the risk they could deal with it.

Moss's accident showed that when the car broke they were only in charge of the 5%. Drivers could imagine they were in command because they were so dextrous, and because they were driving cleverly-made cars. Yet here was their exemplar nearly killed in a car designed by the best and cleverest engineer in the world with the possible exception of those working for the Scuderia Ferrari.

Motor racing's centre of pressure had not yet moved wholesale to the United Kingdom. It was close, but it had not taken place completely yet.

Clark bust by Hungarian sculptor Gyula Nyro.

More worrying still, it transpired that before Moss's car's shaft broke, two others had already failed. Rob Walker, whose car Moss was driving, knew nothing about them: "Colin must have known that the shafts were suspect but he never told us. One had gone on Stacey's car during testing. Nobody was hurt and it was hushed up. It was caused by a bad piece of machining, not necessarily a bad piece of design, but Chapman must have crossed his fingers and hoped that it would not happen again either to his customer cars of which we had one, or to his works cars, driven by Alan Stacey, Innes Ireland, and Jim Clark."

Innes Ireland may have closed his bedroom door with his customary trepidation at the Belgian Grand Prix of 1960 but as usual he survived to open it again. So did Jim Clark. Alan Stacey did not. During the grand prix he was struck by a bird and knocked unconscious, crashing to his death.

Clermont-Ferrand 1965.
Chapman congratulates Clark after victory, Dick Scammel leans over car.
Yves Debraine's picture catches Bernard Cahier in checked cap, and Chapman's bandaged thumb
after hire-car crash.

Chris Bristow was driving a Cooper-Climax for Yeoman Credit Racing that day, and he did not get back to the bedroom door either. His team leader Harry Schell had died testing a car at Silverstone leaving Chris to lead the team at Spa. A protégé of Stirling Moss, he was a hard driver and was racing against the volatile Willy Mairesse when he crashed through a trackside fence and was decapitated. Mairesse, in his first grand prix for Ferrari had a similar hard-charging style. Bristow took the wrong line into the corner, tried to recover but lost control. The car rolled over and over, before throwing his body on to the track.

Jim Clark was the first to arrive at Burnenville after Bristow, before even any warning flags came out. A marshal dashed into the road waving his arms while another ran to grab something lying by the roadside. "It looked like a rag doll," wrote Clark. "It was horrible. I'll never forget the sight of his body being dragged to the side. I found afterwards that my car was spattered with blood."

Clark almost gave up racing on the spot. He wanted to get as far away from cars as possible but once again he enjoined his accident amnesia to see him through. "Your mind begins to function again and slowly everyday things start to crowd their way back. I don't think I am callous but I have been blessed with a bad memory for such things. A day later you feel a little better, three days later you start packing your bags for another race. You keep telling yourself that you must overcome emotion, for at their height

Chapman supervises work on car at Zandvoort, 1962.

your emotions can wield great power over your body and your mind. You can make rash decisions and you have to live with them until you regain your self control. You assume the burden in your own mind even though it was not your fault. It is a kind of guilt by association and you don't initially realise what everyone in such a predicament should realise — no matter how you feel you still have to come back to reality and the living world."

The death of Clark's team mate Alan Stacey had a harrowing effect. His car caught fire and was burnt out, but Clark was thankful that he did not witness the accident. "I was only told about it at the end of the race. If I had seen this accident right after Bristow's I would have retired from motor racing for good." Getting "back to reality" was growing more difficult with every such incident.

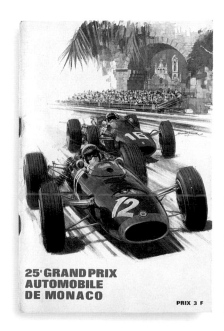

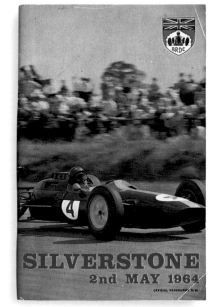

Stewart's BRM and Bandini's Ferrari feature on Monaco race programme for 1967. Bandini crashed in race and died from burns.
Clark won 1962 British Grand Prix at Aintree in a Lotus 25, but engine lasted only ten laps in the 1964 BRDC "May" Silverstone. John Surtees led TT at Goodwood until Clark swept him off track with his Aston Martin.

Admonition for Michael Cooper leaning over track edge at Spa.
Treasured souvenir signed Jim Clark.
He probably did mean it.

Clark had only known Stacey a year and admired his courage for racing despite having lost his right leg below the knee in a motorcycling accident. He was unable to operate all three pedals at once as racing drivers do when braking and changing down for a corner, turning the right ankle to press brake and throttle. He had a twist grip control on the gear lever so that he could change gear and rev the engine at the same time. He compared notes with Clark, who found him congenial company and would join in the game of distracting doctors at race organisers' medical checkups. Stacey would cross his left leg over his artificial one for the knee reflex test, the doctor would tap it, then somebody would ask some pointless question while Stacey gave a little shuffle which still left his good leg ready to respond to the next tap.

On the opposite side of the track from Moss's accident, Mike Taylor crashed when the steering column of his Lotus broke. Taylor's car flew off the road and he suffered broken ribs, a broken collarbone, and an injury to his neck. Phil Hill, world champion in 1961 following the accident to von Trips was among many drivers who criticised the light, apparently flimsy way that Lotuses were made, and vowed never to drive anything so fragile, "Because you never knew what was going to fall off next."

Five Lotuses were entered for Spa and Clark's was the only one running at the end. Of the five drivers, two were badly injured in hospital and one was dead. Ireland was shaken after a lurid spin had sent his car crashing off the road. Clark finished fifth in only his second grand prix. "Coming fifth meant absolutely nothing. I couldn't have cared less."

Although neither Stacey's nor Bristow's accidents were as a result of failures on their cars, Moss's and Taylor's clearly were. Lotus's distressing reputation was further influenced by the crash, soon after Spa, of Jonathan Sieff at Le Mans. An heir to the Marks & Spencer fortune, Sieff was headline news when he crashed practising for the 24 Hours race. For days his life hung in the balance.

Sieff had been going to drive a new 2.0-litre Lotus Elite with Innes Ireland as a replacement for the injured Mike Taylor but, as a result of a mechanic's failure to put a locknut on a tyre valve of Sieff's own slower car, he was thrown out on the fastest part of the course and hurled over a wall. The cause of the crash was not known at first, but following the Spa tragedies it had all the appearance of another Lotus light-weight failure.

Monaco, 1966. Clark on glistening track acknowledges tall photographer David Phipps overhead.

Innes Ireland followed the badly injured Sieff to hospital and the events of the week affected him profoundly. Stacey was dead, Mike Taylor and Moss badly injured, and he confessed to "depths of appalling depression". Normally ebullient, Ireland turned down the Le Mans drive that was on offer and went home.

What was going through Jim Clark's mind?

Chapman saw his exceptional ability, recognised his devotion to the sport, admired his co-ordination and reflexes. When asked what Clark was like, he said he did not subscribe to the old music hall caricature of a Scotsman, but the Scottish trait that did come through was a certain dourness and a strong determination to succeed.

When Chapman said Clark was not mean or "canny", what he may have meant was that his driver's profit motive was less highly developed than his own. He described Clark as intelligent, quick to learn and, notably, he said he had, "a very good memory for things he wishes to remember". Chapman must have noticed what a bad one he had for anything he wanted to forget.

Spa, 1964. Lotus 33. Third victory in a row.

In the first three years he drove for Lotus, Clark devoted himself totally to the job, but after that Chapman found him relaxing, which tended to make him a more measured performer. Stirling Moss reached his peak after he stopped concentrating obsessively on racing, and Chapman expected the same to happen with Clark.

Clark said that after four or five years with Lotus he felt the utmost faith in Chapman and the mechanics and pretty secure, although when he said that he was careful to add, "most of the time". He acknowledged that he had been tempted to leave Lotus, and even been advised by friends to do so. Perhaps if the new, promising, and powerful Ford-Cosworth DFV engine had not been waiting in the wings Clark might have been tempted elsewhere. Stewart felt that Chapman was going to have trouble with him.

Enzo Ferrari discovered that a change was taking place in Jim's outlook. Even after the arrival of the Ford engine, Clark's allegiance to Lotus was not unquestioning; their frailties were having their effect and he was

Author voted Clark
Guild of Motoring Writers'
Driver of the Year
every year.

no longer winning the way he used to. The Ferrari team manager, Franco Lini, learned from a journalist at the 1967 Mexican Grand Prix that Jim Clark might be tempted away. Lini telephoned to Ferrari at once, but met with the cynical response that Clark was merely trying to raise the stakes for his following year's contract with Chapman.

He did not know Jim Clark. It would not have occurred to him to play off one team against another.

Instead Clark was remembering incidents such as a steering breakage in 1963 at Trenton, New Jersey with an Indy car. Chapman not only changed the steering layout on that car but went back to Europe and changed it on all the Formula 1 cars – at least the works cars – even though they had been running for five years without mishap. He would do anything to reassure his drivers although he knew in the end that what reassured drivers most was his almost matchless ability to produce winning cars.

Chapman never knowingly imperilled anybody in one of his racing cars, but engineers have suggested that the design risks he ran were at times biased more towards race-winning than they were towards security. Perhaps this was a penalty of making such swift progress in racing car design but it may have reached a point where even the great Jim Clark, if he was prepared to drive at ten-tenths, or even nine-tenths, did so only with growing anxiety. He said that to have the confidence needed to drive a car to its limit, it was necessary to trust its engineer. He said to Chapman: "Build a car that is going to hang together, and I'll drive it. But if I think it is going to fall to bits, I am going to be two seconds a lap slower."

The Grand Prix Formula 1 of January 1, 1961, limited engine capacity to 1.5 litres unsupercharged, and represented an upgrade of the old Formula 2. For three years there was no second formula because the authorities were reluctant to impose even smaller single-seaters on racing. In 1964 a new Formula 2 was introduced for 1,000cc unsupercharged cars weighing 420kg (926lbs).

South African Grand Prix 1962
Clark and Hill race for the world title.

Clark pulls face for David Phipps, photographer
close to Lotus, close to Chapman, close to Clark.

RELATIVE VALUES

By the time Jim Clark was a successful grand prix driver his self-doubts about his driving had disappeared. If they lingered he was capable of putting anybody right who harboured any doubts. Jabby Crombac was in a car after a race at Pau in France when Jim was taking some people round the street course good-naturedly, sliding on the corners to show them the racing line: "Somebody said, 'Careful Jimmy, you're going to lose it'. He was furious. It was the wrong thing to say. He went even quicker, declaring, 'I'll show you that I won't lose it'. Sometimes the tiger in Jimmy went on the rampage."

Jim's driving was one of the forbidden subjects. He may not have known precisely what it was that gave him such an advantage over his adversaries. All he knew was that everybody else seemed slow; it was almost as though discussing what gift or skill he might have would cause it to leak mysteriously away. So long as he knew he was superior he could talk about driving, but only with those who were not on his level.

When Jackie Stewart started racing he asked Jim for advice, which was given freely and generously. They shared John Whitmore's flat in Balfour Place, in the West End of London, they were practically living together, they raced against one another in Lotus Elites and Jim gave Jackie substantial help in obtaining choice drives with good teams. But providing tips was the limit. At Silverstone Jim abruptly became tight-lipped about braking distances. There was no dialogue. Stewart asked: "Where do you brake for Becketts?" There came no reply. It was some consolation to know that the world champion regarded him as competition, but it signified that there were some topics that were proscribed, not up for debate, not mentioned.

He discovered what Scott Watson had long known, what Jabby Crombac had to discover, what Graham Gauld knew, what I had come to realise, that if you wanted to remain on agreeable terms with Jim Clark you did not probe or question him on what he did not want to reveal.

Sally Swart recalled: "Jimmy could cut off, he really could. There were two totally different portions of his life, the driving and the rest of it. The total concentration went into the driving, the rest of it was nail-biting. He didn't show much sign of nerves. He wasn't different from anyone else. But when he stepped out of the car that was a sign for his indecisiveness to take over. When he got into a car again he was the total master and he never thought of decisions."

He was at his happiest and most relaxed driving on the road, not on the track. He seemed carefree and master of the situation. He was happy at parties with people he knew well where he felt he could let his hair down. He was delighted when he was in Scotland driving on the roomy, beautiful roads he knew well in the countryside that was such a favourite with so many of his countrymen from Sir Walter Scott on.

Still, racing every weekend was important for him to keep in practice. He felt he might lose his edge if he missed a race. It kept his eye in. Once he realised his capabilities racing on a regular basis seemed to reassure him. He felt he had no need to pick dog fights with anyone because he was so superior. It came easily. All he had to do was refine the abilities he already had, make them seem almost effortless.

Chapman tried to analyse his talent, but could only say that he had every essential ingredient for a racing driver physically and mentally that he could imagine. Clark's reputation as a test driver was thought faulty because he would adjust his driving to suit any inconsistency in the car. Like the engaging Swede, Ronnie Peterson and some others with great natural talent, this was true to some extent but Chapman, skilled driver himself, could assimilate the information Clark gave him. He understood Clark perfectly. Clark would never tell him to tighten up a roll bar or adjust the brake balance of the car. He would report what it felt like to drive and Chapman would know exactly what he meant. Their communication was precise, flawless, explicit, and it bred consummate cars.

Jim with sisters Mattie, Isobel, Susan and their mother.

For his part Chapman never told Clark how to drive. It was part of their understanding. Each had his own domain; they would tell each other what was going on, but never interfere with the other's side of the business.

Non-interference was the key ingredient in Clark's personal affairs as well. Jabby Crombac met him at Le Mans when he went to drive the Elite in 1959. Already close to Lotus,

Crombac stayed in the hotel Chez Monsieur Meitcar, Auberge St Nicholas, in Mayet. As Lotus's man on the Continent he was the link in the sometimes fractured relationship between Chapman and the Automobile Club de l'Ouest which organised the 24 Hours race, handling the entries when there were more applicants than places. He knew ways and means of obtaining entries which Chapman, who could not speak French, would have had difficulty obtaining on his own.

Jim struck Crombac as pleasant, but subdued. As they grew closer he was impressed with Clark's genuine modesty but startled at his prudishness. On one occasion at Rheims he was with the sister of another British driver, and Crombac was astonished to find she had to stay in a different hotel. Clark would only meet her after dark when nobody could see him going to her room.

What a contrast to the older Clark when his outlook towards girls seemed to change for the worse. After the agreeable years with Sally he grew less compassionate, treating them less charitably. It might even have been another consequence of his relationship with Chapman. Racing to Chapman was a religion. Nothing was allowed to stand in its way and Jim probably never realised how devious, cunning, astute, and brilliantly clever Chapman was at keeping him disciplined.

He would do anything to keep Clark happy, content, soothed – and in the team. When he was running Jim's affairs, Scott Watson became a member of the Lotus family. When Jim was with Sally, she was too, keeping lap charts, sitting on the pit counter with Hazel Chapman. But once Scott Watson seemed in the way, he soon became redundant. Did Chapman play a role in his dismissal? Who knows.

Chapman may have unwittingly affected Jimmy's attitude to women. As one of the most respected individuals in motor racing, with matinee idol looks, to say nothing of his power, influence and quick, dry wit, Chapman was immensely attractive to women. Although he remained happily married to Hazel, the temptation to have affairs must have been almost irresistible.

It was a mark of his strong, practically overpowering personality that he commanded prodigious loyalty among people who were associated with him. He was Clark's Svengali. The brilliance of a dialogue with Chapman made anybody feel consequential, erudite, a member of the Lotus inner circle, and if Chapman was its centre, Jim Clark was its keystone.

He could scarcely avoid picking up some of Chapman's debonair,

World travellers Jackie and Helen Stewart, Sally Stokes and Jim Clark,
Bette and Graham Hill.

easy-going, style. Since Chapman knew marriage could unsettle his favourite driver and might even make him give up racing altogether, he was unlikely to have encouraged the idea. What effect did that have on Jim's decision not to marry while he was racing? Who knows.

Sally was the longest-lasting love of Jim Clark's life. Beautiful, petite, she was in great demand for car advertisements because she made the cars look big. The archetypal English girl to the tips of her exquisitely manicured and well-bred fingers, she loved horses, mixed well among the motor racing crowd and when she met Jim Clark it seemed the perfect match.

She travelled with him, sat on the pit counter, yet was clever enough to know when to make herself scarce. There are not many photographs of them them together at races because Jim avoided being photographed with her. "Other girls went up to their boyfriends or husbands after a victory and flung their arms around his neck to be in the photo. I never did, ever. I felt I wasn't welcome there. If he was being photographed I was careful to keep out of it. He told me he did not want his parents to get the wrong idea." Jim wanted to keep a clean profile, and show his friends in Scotland that he was working hard at his racing, not being a playboy surrounded by pretty young women: "He was very careful how he was photographed and with whom. I suppose all of us suffered from that a bit."

Prompted by Chapman, Jim Clark took up flying. He did not need an aeroplane, but wanted one for the freedom, (once again the all-important psychological control) it gave him. He enjoyed the sensations of flying just as he enjoyed the sensations of driving a racing car. He managed flight planning and navigation well for a supposed non-achiever at school.

Sally flew in his aeroplane, sometimes anxiously. Her father was a senior officer in the Royal Air Force and she knew the perils. Jim enjoyed flying although he had his quota of uneasy moments. On one of his first solo flights he took off from Luton, put a road map on Sally's knee and said: "I've got to get to Pau. Head south, try to find a Route Nationale and we'll go down that." They managed to get over the Channel, followed some railway lines and, to their relief, found Pau.

As they were leaving afterwards a towering thunderstorm loomed overhead and Jim was more tense than he would admit, but he was as proud of bringing his aircraft successfully back to England as he had been winning the race. Flying safely was a real challenge.

He bought a new aeroplane in America but it was lost on the way across the Atlantic. It either crashed, or was stolen and may have been taken

Jim's Piper Twin Comanche.
Two 160bhp Avco Lycomings, 205mph; 20,000ft ceiling;
range 1,110 miles. Ex-Chapman.

to some place like Cuba. He had bad luck with things like that. Ford exchanged the Plymouth Sports Fury which was the Indy pace car, part of his prize for winning in 1965 for a Mustang which fell on to the quay at Southampton docks. He was very upset. So was Ford because it could not get another one and asked him to accept a Galaxie instead like the one they were giving Colin Chapman. He was sad that he never got the Mustang, although he had a lot of fun in the Galaxie, especially in London.

Clark and Chapman flew to European meetings, often landing close to the track, and in 1965 just after they had won Indy, flew to Clermont Ferrand for the French Grand Prix. It took four hours and Chapman had had a stressful time with a lot of last minute decisions. When they landed in the late afternoon they found something of a party in progress at Clermont's little airport and picking up their hire car, were invited by the mayor and corporation to meet Yuri Gagarin the world's first astronaut. He had flown in from the air show at Le Bourget to a civic reception with a lot of Russians. The Lotus team was introduced, but the translators did not make a very good job. Gagarin shook hands, smiled politely and sat down.

They were enjoying the champagne when the astronaut realised he had just met Jim Clark. He leapt from his chair, came over, hugged and kissed Jim and Chapman, and told them he was an avid fan. He knew all about Indy, apologised profusely, and asked them to sit down and talk.

Gagarin made his flight in space in April 1961, and died on March 27 1968 when his MiG-15 jet trainer crashed near Moscow barely 10 days before Jim Clark's accident at Hockenheim.

The meeting with Gagarin was memorable, but too much champagne flowed and Chapman got into the hire car, an old Peugeot. He was only half looking where he was going, and half trying to read a map. They had not been booked in at their usual Post Hotel, so Sally navigated while in his usual robust style Chapman swung through the bends. A few kilometres into the hills he failed to negotiate a corner, the Peugeot went into a ditch and came to a jarring halt. Chapman suffered a cut thumb, Sally went through the windscreen, while Jim was thrown on to the front seat, covered in glass.

Mike Spence in the back was unhurt. They got out with Chapman moaning about his thumb, Jim promptly fainted, while Sally had blood pouring from cuts to her head and face. She remembered thinking. "What do you do with somebody who's fainted?" and tried to pick Jim up and stuff his head between his knees. He revived sufficiently to berate her for spilling blood all over his suit. "That's gratitude," she thought.

Worse was to come. Chapman was determined the press must not know about the accident, so Sally was bundled back into the Peugeot, still driveable, to steer it while Mike Spence helped to push it out of the ditch. Sally was not accustomed to right hand drive, and when it was heaved backwards she could not find the brake in the darkness. The car rolled gently in reverse until Chapman yelled in alarm and Sally found the pedal just in time to prevent the car plunging into a ravine.

They drove back to their regular hotel, wrapped scarves round Sally's head, went to a surgery at midnight after everybody else had gone to bed, and were still being stitched up at 3am. As his price for silence the doctor was invited to the pits, and watched Jim Clark win the French Grand Prix.

The press did find out. Patrick Mennem knew, but as a sporting gesture like the other journalist members of the grand prix circus, somehow forgot to file the story.

Within a few years Gagarin, Clark, Spence, and Chapman were gone. Sally, none the worse for her ordeal, became the only survivor.

Jim worried that beautiful, slim, sophisticated model-girl Sally was part of his motor racing life and might not adapt to being back on the farm. Quite probably she would have, given her devotion to horses and liking for country life. She certainly showed great forbearance in moments of crisis.

Why he and Sally split up is no mystery. She gave him an ultimatum about making their relationship permanent and he was not disposed to do so. He told her to go ahead and marry somebody else, even if it hurt him, and after that he was unlikely to make the essential commitment to any girl.

When Sally mentioned marriage, overnight she was gone. He had plenty of girlfriends, some he would keep for two days, in Paris. The girls were queuing up. Jabby Crombac said he was careful never to pick up a girl after him: "Once she had been touched by him she was sacrosanct."

Walter Hayes felt that one of the reasons he did not marry Sally was that he had could never think beyond the year

Colin Chapman adopted Clark-style headgear.

Girl in pearls. Sally Swart, nee Stokes.

he was in. "Sally's mistake was to make him jealous, and he didn't get jealous, he just got mad. He never ever talked about doing anything else but motor racing. He never showed any interest in private business. So far as the future was concerned he was going to marry Sally, but he didn't know when, maybe he'd think about it next year. He used to say that the sport was too dangerous for him to get married. He didn't always say it publicly but he did say it to me, so I said why don't you tell Sally. I once asked Sally, 'When are you going to get married?' and she said 'You ask him.' So I said to him, 'Why don't you just tell her that you are going to marry her, but you would like your motor racing career to come to an end first?' But he never did."

Jim Clark was pursued by many girls. Sometimes it upset him, sometimes it amused him, but he accepted it with good grace and responded in the way that any young man with a strong libido and a sense of humour would. His encounters were many and varied, although he lost some respect for women because of the way they behaved. Jabby Crombac described how after races girls would walk up and down in front of the motorhome. "He only had to smile or make a little move and one would come and he would take her out for dinner and then she would be his – to keep if he wanted."

Andrew Ferguson, the Lotus racing manager recalled an occasion at Indianapolis when Chapman came down to breakfast. He and Jim were sharing a room, and he was in what Ferguson called a "quivering lower lip"mood. Ferguson enquired what was wrong. "You know I don't sleep well. Well Jimmy went out on his own last night, and I was woken up by him coming back into the room with some bird. I had to pretend to be asleep, and they went into the bathroom. I couldn't believe it. They had a noisy shower together, then they both got into Jimmy's bed. By this time I was not very happy."

"Then she said, 'What about him – won't we wake him up?' And do you know what Jimmy said? 'Don't worry about him – the silly bugger never wakes up.' God knows what time I got to sleep."

Jimmy asked Ferguson in future to reserve him a single room.

Many girls came on the scene and most of them went as quickly as they arrived. Kate Eccles was another love of his life and although she may

Icons of the 1960s.
Model Jean Shrimpton, racing driver Jim Clark, and Ford Corsair.

Photograph David Bailey.

have thought she was the only one at that time, she probably was not. There were plenty who thought they were the only ones too.

Yet Kate in a way was a success. She was a girl in a different mould. She was not overwhelmed just because he was Jim Clark. She was her own woman and it was perhaps the first time that he met a girl who would stand up to him. "You knew he was hooked on Kate," said Crombac. Jim Clark would drink to be social, but abhorred smoking which would surely have led to problems if he had lived further into the John Player era at Lotus. Sally never smoked when she was with Jimmy, but Kate chain-smoked and when Jimmy asked her to stop she refused. "I think that was what did the trick," said Jabby.

Jim's girlfriends tended to be blonde, slim, and pretty, and many bore a striking resemblance to Sally. Friends would remark on it and call them, not unkindly, Sally Mark VI or Sally Mark VII. The consensus among other women close to him was that he should have married Sally, and although she married Ed Swart and lived happily ever after, she never forgot Jim Clark. Helen Stewart recalled: "There were a lot of bad times for her that she probably doesn't remember. When he wouldn't marry her, she got very angry and depressed. They'd been together a long time. She took care of him, she did everything for him. Why he couldn't make that decision, I don't know. Maybe he felt she was too much of a Londoner, a southerner, a sophisticate. When they were living in London or went up to the farm she would cook for him, do anything a wife would do. But she wasn't a wife and she resented that."

Jim could be unchivalrous. In Spain with a girl he had been seeing a lot of, a journalist asked: "Is this your girlfriend? Are you going to marry her?" He was coldly dismissive: "She's just a girl." Some women complained that towards the end of his life the veneer of charm was thin, the politeness all but gone.

Jackie Stewart thought Jim afraid of women and certainly afraid of making commitments to them. Once again Jim's worries about being exploited resurfaced. He repeatedly thought people were trying to take advantage of him and it was sometimes the same with girls. "He spent a lot of time with them, and he wanted them to adore him and to love him, and be available for him but he did not want to commit to them. He was really insecure."

It was a further example of the Jim Clark dichotomy. He was careful to keep his two lives apart, and constantly fretted over his image in the press. He did not want to give up the sweet life to which he was growing

accustomed. He did not want to break the spell and much as he loved his home and family, and much as he was careful to nurture his image, he did not think he was quite ready to rejoin them.

Perhaps Jim Clark was really like all racing drivers, as Derek Bell recounted, and they all have to repress their emotions. Walter Hayes, as ever, had a theory: "They all try to develop another personality. When I first met Niki Lauda he was just a lad driving Cortinas in Austria. Later he had to have a new business career notwithstanding the trauma of his terrible accident. They all need to have a second personality because the first one becomes uncomfortable to live with."

"Graham Hill was a great driver. Nobody will ever persuade me that he wasn't. I doubt if anybody else had more true grit and determination, yet Graham was a man full of self-doubts, because his evident public face, and his ability at public speaking concealed, as with Jackie Stewart, great nervousness underneath. You can see by the way Jackie keeps chasing the world, chasing people, chasing things to do and really was quite frightened of retirement. It was as though he had this compulsion about not being left alone. They're not altogether normal people. It's dangerous to go around psychologising, but it's truer of people than you think."

When he shared a flat in Paris with Crombac yet another Jim Clark emerged. He became more comfortable with himself, and more relaxed living in a world where people did not harass him. He did not need to play the role of the Border farmer or suffer any of the disadvantages of being a celebrity. He lived a cosmopolitan existence and spent much time with the wealthy Michel Finquel who introduced him to a string of girlfriends.

Walter Hayes wished Jabby had not encouraged him to spend so much time in Paris and if only he had realised that the money was not all that important, and that he'd stayed in England it would have been better. "He became a bit disconnected then you know. There were no faxes or anything like that and he was a terrible letter writer, and so on the whole that period in Paris was not just tax exile, it was exile."

Most people who knew him well, like Helen Stewart, found Jim straightforward but had reservations about his moods. Motor racing may have been his way of making money doing something he enjoyed, but he seldom confided in her. "He would talk to me about his girlfriends, but that would make him bite his nails more than anything."

There were still aspects nobody quite understood. Stewart by contrast was outgoing and Clark enjoyed his company. Their dissimilarity made Jim appear reserved. "He might have been concealing an arrogant streak, and

Clark's blue Bell helmet plain, modest, unadorned.
White peak added in mid-career when better-managed
slipstream reduced buffetting.

was really more self-possessed than he seemed," was how one old friend put it.

He had a lively sense of fun but probably because of his uncommunicative nature his reputation for being rather serious persisted. There may have been a certain Scottish dourness about him, yet he laughed a great deal. When he died somebody asked Graham Hill what he would miss most about Jim Clark and he replied: "His smile. It lit up his whole face." It did, and partly because he was Jimmy Clark people joined in. He could light up a whole room and even laugh at himself if the barb was not too sharp.

Jim Clark had few disputes with fellow drivers, but one which smouldered for years was with his fellow-Scot Innes Ireland. Robert McGregor Innes Ireland, son of a Kirkudbright vet, started racing in 1952 but it was four years before he struck success with a Lotus XI. He drove for Ecurie Ecosse and joined Team Lotus in 1959.

It had the best car, but victory for the inexperienced works team was delayed until the final race of 1961 when, after three years' trying, Ireland won the American Grand Prix.

He was fired by Colin Chapman almost at once. For 1962 there was to be a new car, the revolutionary Lotus 25 and a new team leader, Jim Clark. Ireland felt that Jim had somehow edged him out. Chapman regarded Innes as lucky to have been in the team in the first place. He had enjoyed the fruits of the first rear engined Lotus and beat Moss twice in one day at the spring meeting at Goodwood. But Chapman felt he knew where the credit was due; it was down to his car more than Innes's driving.

To Jim Clark, Innes represented another kind of Scotsman, who could get embarrassingly drunk, and send the wrong messages on motor racing back to Scotland. Ireland suffered the indignity of being told at the London motor show by Geoff Murdoch of Esso that he should enquire about his future with Chapman, who looked at his feet and said he would not be required in 1962. He was not even included in the team for the final non-championship races of the season in South Africa – the Rand Grand Prix, the Natal Grand Prix, and the South African Grand Prix, all won by Jim Clark in a Lotus 21.

It was a crushing blow which affected Ireland all his life. He remained immensely popular and thoroughly likeable, particularly in his later years throughout a tragic personal history. He never won another grand prix although he raced until 1966, and never really forgave Jim Clark although in public both men tried to conceal their mutual distaste.

Ireland made his own way to the 1962 South African races, arriving at the track for practice after partying into the small hours with Gregor Grant. Clark disapproved strongly. He did not want to be on the same track. Innes was hostile towards Jim, who could be just as belligerent in return and never made any effort to put things right. He was rarely more than polite with Ireland, unlike Trevor Taylor who was also in the Lotus team for 1962 but who made a point of soothing Innes's bruised feelings.

Jim Clark never knowingly endangered another driver on the track, but he had his own subtle way of dealing with Ireland's animosity. Graham Gauld recalled the occasion.

"At the Italian Grand Prix, Monza 1964, Jim was in the lead, being harried by Dan Gurney in the Brabham. They came up to lap Innes at the end of the straight, and Jimmy did the usual, stuck his nose in on the approach to the corner. Innes wasn't having that and cut right across. Jim pulled back. He said, 'I went round the rest of the lap wondering what to do. I had Dan right behind me and the next time we came into the corner I just sat right back and watched Innes, and waited until I saw him glance in his mirrors. As soon as he did that I lifted off, and of course Dan shot past me and went for the inside. Innes saw a nosecone coming up the inside, thought it was me and chopped across again. But of course nobody does that to Dan Gurney, and while both of them were wobbling I went round the outside'."

Clark's dispute with Innes Ireland, and his off-hand treatment of Ian Scott Watson who had played such a pivotal role in launching his career, are well known, but he could also be brittle in other relationships, even to people with whom he was quite familiar, both professionally and socially. They found, as I did, the contentious matters into which it was unwise to stray, − money, girlfriends, and the emotional side of motor racing.

Clark's nail biting betrayed his tension, his repression of his deep anxiety about motor racing. Yet he rarely talked openly to anyone about the risks except in the way he did after the steering fault at Trenton.

He told David Benson what it was like to race at a mile oval track, nose to tail at 180-185 mph. The cars had metal fenders round the gearbox at the back, and one became detached from the car in front. It bounced on

Wives in pits at Zandvoort.
From left Nina Rindt, Sally Courage, Patty McLaren, widows all by
year's end 1970. With Bette Hill and Helen Stewart.

the road and struck the front of Clark's car to his acute indignation. Benson said: "He looked at me in disbelief and said, 'You know David, if it had bounced a little higher, it could have killed me'. It seemed he'd never thought about it."

He probably had. Few people ever recall Jim Clark talking about the perils of his profession. He never spoke about the von Trips accident yet we know it affected him profoundly; look at the detail he went into, devoting an entire chapter to it in his 1964 book *At The Wheel*. Recall the anxiety he displayed when he went home to his sisters. Consider the pressure brought about by the Italian police investigations, and the way he fielded questions at press conferences. The repression of his feelings that he called self-control continued throughout his career and changed him profoundly so that by 1968 there was not much left of the shy Border farmer.

Some people were sure he did not believe he would be killed in a racing car. He knew he had such mastery, such talent, that he did not understand why other drivers were not as quick as he was and although he seemed not to understand what it was that gave him this superiority, he knew he had it, and he knew he had to rely on it to survive.

He knew it was not entirely due to the design of the cars with which Chapman was supplying him, because there were enough other drivers in Lotuses who would have kept up with him if they had been able. There is an analogy here with the late Ayrton Senna who believed quite sincerely that he had a God-given gift that would see him through. In the end it failed him too.

Was Jim Clark sharing his confidence that he felt safe in a racing car because that was what he wanted to believe? It looks as though his anxiety about the final outcome of his motor racing career increased as the years passed, yet he stifled it. Other drivers could mention what was to Jim Clark unmentionable. He had a superstition about it. If it was not talked about perhaps it was impossible.

The effects of Scott Watson's friendship with Clark were far-reaching and long-standing, even though it ended in harsh words and bruised feelings, yet for the most part Clark inspired loyalty and affection among his friends apparently effortlessly. It was a family trait. His sisters have a similar rare charm and dignity which has the same disarming result.

For Jim it was a characteristic that could be an occasional embarrassment when he was still new to celebrity status. He did not know how to detach himself from unwelcome fans, hero-worshippers, motor racing groupies of either sex, or very occasionally professional Scots over-anxious to establish kinship. These he dreaded, worried lest they take word back to Scotland that Jim Clark had grown too big for his boots. Such denunciation might all too easily get back to a close-knit Border community, a close-knit family, and create trouble.

On the other hand it was sometimes convenient to be well known. He eventually acquired the knack of dealing with unwanted scrutiny – once he had taken on the appearance of an extrovert true to the psychiatric assessment and even managed to make a decent speech in public instead of stammering a brief and dutiful "thank-you". As he found himself more in control socially, he could move more easily, the spring in his step grew more natural, and the tightness in his shoulders that Jackie Stewart recognised as the mannerism of someone suppressing emotion became looser.

Grande vitesse, haute couture. Jochen and Nina Rindt.

More surprising, despite his complete mastery of his fellow-drivers they regarded him almost to a man with real affection. Trevor Taylor, who drove with him in the Lotus team, told *Motor Sport*: "We were very very good friends. He shared information on the car. He was a good lad." To be known chiefly as Jim Clark's team-mate never rankled with Taylor. "We shared the Formula Junior championship in 1960 and when Jimmy moved to Formula 1, I won the Junior championship again in 1961. There was no sort of bitchiness between us. We used to share hotel rooms and I used to go and stay with him at home. Jimmy Clark was never a bighead. He would never speak loudly to anybody. He was brilliant, but he needed company."

Flashback to Formula Junior. Jim Clark and Trevor Taylor.

Yet it was Trevor Taylor who first spotted the anxious Clark: "We were testing at Oulton Park when he had a radius arm break on the Formula 1 car. They were only single shear and he was getting a little bit twitchy, a little bit nervous. We spoke that night in the hotel and he said, 'Trevor, I never know what the hell's going to break next.' That wasn't Jimmy. He wasn't that type of chap. He'd get in a car and off he'd go."

Jackie Stewart recounts a visit to Bermuda he and Helen made with Jochen and Nina Rindt and Jim and Sally. "We went on holiday to this apartment which he was then spending a bit of time in, and found it was barely furnished. Jimmy went out with Helen to buy some furnishings, and didn't want to pay for them. It was amazing. It was for his house. We told him some things were needed and should we buy them and he said yes. And then afterwards he'd say, 'Well, I don't know if we needed that, I don't want to pay for that'. He had an amazing ability to avoid dealing with things." Stewart had a view that he did not actually want to deal with a lot of things in life.

During the 1967 holiday in Bermuda, Jim took a call from Bill France, organiser of the NASCAR stock car series. Would be come with his friend Jackie Stewart to compete in a race at Rockingham? Jim asked Jackie, who wanted to know the financial arrangements, and whether the car would be competitive. He was concerned about the financial aspect, and did not want to risk racing round at the back of the field. He knew that race organisers wanted international celebrities to boost attendance and was not prepared to give them the commercial advantages of appearing without suitable arrangements.

Clark was also a winner in Formula 2 against 'old Jack Brabham'.

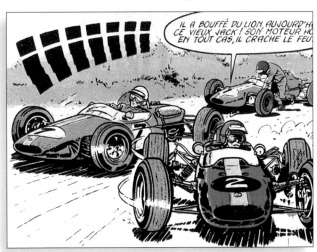

Jim said he didn't think Jackie would come, but his other friend Jochen Rindt just might. The pair left the following morning and although Rindt did not race, Jim did. His inquisitiveness led him to try all sorts of cars. Shortly before his death he drove a turbine-powered Lotus 56 at Indianapolis. He came back to Europe telling Jabby Crombac he had driven the next car to win at Indy. Parnelli Jones nearly made his prediction true.

Scottish flag in Indiana.
Michael Turner's painting shows saltire in line of banners as Clark takes lead for
1965 victory at 150.686mph.

INDIANAPOLIS

If the key to the American revolution in racing car design was Colin Chapman and Jim Clark unlocked its door, it was Jack Brabham and Dan Gurney who knocked first. Brabham ran a Cooper at Indianapolis in 1961, like the one he had used to win the 1959 and 1960 world championships, providing a broad intimation that the end was nigh for the Speedway's traditional, big front-engined roadsters. In 1962 Gurney drove a mid-engined clone of Brabham's Cooper, but momentously, he invited Colin Chapman along to watch

The potential for a challenge to the Indy roadsters had been recognised by Rodger Ward, winner in 1959, and one of the greatest United States Automobile Club (USAC) racers with 26 victories. In December 1959 in the first United States Grand Prix at Sebring he entered an Offenhauser-engined Kurtis dirt track racer. It was 43 seconds a lap slower than Stirling Moss's Cooper-Climax over the rather unsuitable five mile airfield circuit, where Bruce McLaren became the youngest winner of a world championship race at the age of 22.

Ward drove bravely but the little 1.7 litre Kurtis was outclassed. Deeply impressed with the opposition he had encountered, he

Jackie Stewart on fact-finding visit to American racing, quizzes evasive Clark.

convinced John Cooper and Jack Brabham that they should try their luck at Indianapolis. There was a great deal of money to be won from even a respectable finishing position, so the following October they came straight from racing at Watkins Glen and Riverside for a try-out, and in a car small by comparison with the 4.2 litre Offenhauser-engined roadsters, lapped easily at 143mph, only 3mph slower than the 1960 fastest qualifying lap.

A Cooper could surely be made competitive in time for the 1961 race, although not before Brabham was rebuked by track officials for going so fast. Part of Indy's cryptic code was that Brabham's track record, world titles notwithstanding, counted for nothing when it came to Speedway skill. He soon showed that matching the roadsters with his little 2½ litre mid-engined car was relatively easy, and even though it was slower on the straights, its superior balance and better handling made it faster through the corners than any car in Indianapolis history. It reached 143mph through the turns against the roadsters' 135mph. Not only that, but using AvGas at 12mpg against the roadster's voracious 2-3mpg of alcohol fuel meant fewer stops.

For the conservative Indy establishment it was the end of the old world but for Dan Gurney, already successful in Formula 1, it was the dawn of a new one. He longed to mount a challenge, and when he saw Brabham finishing ninth despite unsatisfactory Dunlop tyres, slightly shaky Cooper technology and unfamiliarity with Indianapolis, he became certain that he could. Gurney's 1962 mid-engined Harvey Aluminum Special was designed by John Crosthwaite, but Gurney knew the best designer in the world was Chapman, and invited him to America. Typically Chapman postponed a decision until the airline ticket arrived.

The Harvey's Buick V-8 employed a modified production cylinder block, so it had less power than the racing Offenhausers, yet the car qualified eighth fastest, and ran among the leading ten until it dropped out at half-distance. Chapman was astonished. Compared with Formula 1, Indianapolis was still in the dark ages technically as features of successful cars were copied year by year, sending designers down false evolutionary trails until the quirky results were quite unlike racing cars anywhere else. Success may have had little to do with offset suspension, or any of the capricious features Indy cars acquired, yet rivals solemnly noted every detail and came up with 'improvements' every year. Design was stagnant and development all but non-existent.

Chapman knew he could demolish the uniformity. He could also see that with $125,000 available in prize money (around £45,000 or £525,000 at 1990s values, and more than Team Lotus could earn in an entire year of Formula 1), it was well worth the effort. What he needed was somebody willing to put up the cash in the first place.

Gurney introduced him to Ford Motor Company in America.

It was a fortunate coincidence. Ford had been thinking about it anyway. Donald Frey and Dave Evans had seen the collapse of the American manufacturers' self-imposed ordinance not to get involved in motor racing; Ford was pursuing a new image after finding that it had a reputation for cars that were worthy but dull. Frey and Evans had been at Indianapolis too; they could see that a revolution was near, knew Chapman's reputation, so as soon as he arrived at Ford's Dearborn

Indy test day.
Jim Clark with Dan Gurney, moving spirit behind Indianapolis Lotuses.

Indy Lotus with offset suspension and veteran Ford racer. Car at rear is 1917 Indianapolis-style Model T racer.

headquarters, he was ushered to the executive suite on the top floor.

Ford had taken part at Indianapolis in 1935, when Harry Miller's strategy was to run ten cars with Ford V-8s. The project started late, only four cars qualified, three soon retired, and the fourth limped round. Ignominy never sat easily on Ford's shoulders and memories of the debâcle lingered.

In 1961 Ford Division's general manager Robert McNamara joined President Kennedy's government as Secretary of Defense (he was later President of the World Bank) and 36 year old Lee Iacocca, an ardent advocate of racing, took his place. Hardware was already waiting in the wings. Harley Copp, an executive with a wide-ranging brief for engineering, commissioned work in 1956 on a 32-valve racing V-8, and even though Ford found Chapman arrogant and difficult, a framework for tackling Indianapolis in 1963 was agreed. Chapman was dismissive of the peculiarities and traditions of the Speedway, he knew he could build a better car and only Gurney's all-American diplomacy saved the day. Lotus embarked on designing a car for the richest race on the calendar.

Andrew Ferguson explained the position to Jim Clark. He was to pay his hotel and airline expenses from his $5,000 retainer and take his usual share, 45 per cent, of any winnings. It was an offer, Chapman suggested to Ferguson, that he could not refuse.

Unexpectedly he did. He asked for an agreement in writing that Lotus would be responsible for his expenses. It did not last. Chapman managed to make him pay in later years.

Immediately after the American Grand Prix at Watkins Glen in October, Trevor Taylor's Formula 1 car was taken to Indianapolis where, despite it being 1½ litres against Brabham's Cooper's 2½ it still did 143mph; once again it was faster through the turns than the regular roadsters, although like Brabham Clark was unimpressed with the mandatory rookie test aimed at weeding out inexperienced or unsatisfactory drivers. The USAC observers were astonished at how he achieved the exact speeds required for each incremental level. "The only problem came when the car wobbled a bit exiting Turn Four," said Dick Scammell. "They started to make a fuss about that but Jimmy just said calmly, `A rabbit ran across the track. I didn't want to hit it.'"

The design of an Indianapolis Lotus crystallised as a larger version of

the grand prix Lotus 25, with a Ford V-8 engine and sufficient length to accommodate 6ft 2in of Dan Gurney.

When qualifying began on 6th May, the speed of the Lotus-Fords electrified the Indy establishment. Gurney was lapping so fast, 149mph, that rivals complained to Firestone about the 15-inch tyres he was using. There was much commotion about safety as startled teams sought ways of combating the assault on what they regarded as their birthright. The Chapman design and the skill of Clark and Gurney threatened to eclipse them.

Had it not been for the infamous episode in the closing stages of the race, when the Watson-Offenhauser of Parnelli Jones in the lead sprayed so much oil on the track that Clark was certain it would be black-flagged off the course, the Lotus would have won. Jim Clark was scrupulous in his obedience to the Speedway's rules but in this instance the Speedway let him down. Jones's oil stained not only the track, but the reputation of American racing although characteristically Jim called Jones's performance a "…damn fine drive". He could afford to be magnanimous. He had just won 45 per cent of $55,238, more than any foreign driver had ever taken home from Indiana.

Ford was disappointed at the outcome but not put out. Sporting America knew that Clark was the moral winner, and Lotus undertook to race in two end-of-season events at Milwaukee, Wisconsin, in August and Trenton in September. US racing politicians tried to procure changes in the regulations to outlaw the Lotuses, but at Milwaukee Clark shattered the lap record, won convincingly, and lapped every car in the race except A J Foyt's. At Trenton he was the fastest on the course until mechanical failure intervened, and the brief, spectacular competition career of the Lotus 29 came to an end.

Clark did not win at Indianapolis in 1964 with the Lotus 34, betrayed disastrously and potentially fatally by Chapman's decision to run on Dunlop tyres. Ford paid Team Lotus $46,000 to make three cars, and a $20,000 retainer for attending qualifying on May 1. Clark went out in front of 250,000 people and the atmosphere from 6am when the gates opened was electric. According to Andrew Ferguson his composure throughout the day never changed. "Calm, methodical throughout, he could just as easily have been waiting to drive his Lotus Elite round Brands Hatch."

His qualifying speeds, announced to roars of approval from the huge crowd were 7mph faster than the old record, 158.828mph, with one lap

Jim Clark receives trophy for fastest qualifying lap at 158.828mph in 1964 from Raymond Firestone.
He should have taken the tyres instead.

over 160mph. Clark led the race from pole until a huge accident on the second lap blocked the track with flaming wreckage. Two drivers, Dave McDonald and Eddie Sachs died, several others were badly burned, and the race was stopped while the debris was cleared.

Jim stopped by the pits, hauled himself out of the car and sat on the ground using the left front tyre as a backrest. "Don't look so worried," he said to Ferguson. Then with heavy irony: "It's only a sport."

Out of the 33 starters, 13 were mid-engined, seven with Ford V-8s, six were Offenhausers. There were two front-engined Novi V-8s and the Ferguson-Novi four-wheel-drive car. The remainder were front-engined roadsters. The three cars on the front row of the grid all had four-cam Ford V-8s, Clark with the Lotus 34, Bobby Marshman with one of the previous year's Lotus 29s, and Rodger Ward with an A J Watson mid-engined car. Clark had qualified at 158.828mph over four qualifying laps, his fastest at 159.337mph on alcohol fuel although for the race he used regular petrol like most of the Fords except Rodger Ward's.

Chapman's unwise choice of Dunlops brought disaster.

Clark's Dunlops were not equal to the task. After less than 40 laps the treads stripped off. He came out of Turn Four and the flailing strips of tyre tore into the rear suspension which collapsed, and the left rear wheel broke loose and lay on top of the engine. The failure at the back raised the right front wheel off the track, and Clark was left with only the left one to steer by. The other rear wheel was intact, and the left rear corner dragged along in a shower of sparks. At 150mph he somehow kept the car under control down the straight, slowing as he reached Turn One at the bottom of the banking, and gently guided it on to the grass clear of the traffic.

David Benson found him at the Speedway Motel, sitting in the diner with a hamburger and chips, apparently unmoved. "He told me that he had dared not touch the brakes. The transmission had locked so there was no engine braking on the remaining rear wheel and he had to steer with the utmost delicacy on the remaining front wheel in contact with the road. 'It was fingertips stuff David,' he said with the ends of his fingers on the rim of an imaginary steering wheel."

Once again Clark proved equal to the task. The psychiatric pattern asserted itself. The stress produced the right answer. There was no panic, no confusion. He fed exactly the right signals into the steering wheel through

Indianapolis 1964.
Clark leaps into first gear
and sets two record laps
before multiple accident
eliminates seven cars and
costs two lives.
Jim's mother was so affected
he almost scratched from
following year.

his sensitive fingertips and brought the car to a stop on the infield. He may have said that it was a scary experience, but at the time except for the shot of adrenalin he undoubtedly felt, there was no time for fright. Benson said he felt Jim knew he had control, and as long as no other cars crossed his path he knew he was going to avert disaster. "It was the nearest he ever came with me to analysing how he drove."

His 24th place earned 45 per cent of $12,400, $5,580 or a paltry £2,030, around £20,000 at 1990s prices.

For the following year, 1965, after a deal of argument, Ford's stake in Lotus's Indianapolis programme went up to $147,000 plus $25,000 set aside to cover unexpected costs. There was also $30,000 to be paid by Ford for the winning car − if it won. It was a sound investment, but it was not without further worry.

At a meeting at Cheshunt between Ford and Lotus the budget was hammered out, Ford's first offer of $75,000 was steadily raised to cover the spiralling costs. There were to be three new cars, Ford would supply five new engines, full race-tuned quad-cam units supplied and tended by Ford free of charge.

Complicated arrangements were made for accommodating the drivers' engagements in grands prix and everything seemed finally to have been agreed. Ford was above all intent on having Jim Clark as its number one driver; it saw Lotus not just as the constructors of the cars, but as the means by which Ford would have the services of the best driver in the world.

He was invited to the meeting at which the deal was to be finalised, but said little. Something was worrying him and in due course he was asked what it was.

"It's my mother," he said.

Andrew Ferguson recounted how to the businessmen and engineers planning for the greatest event in motor racing, his reply came with the shock of a thunderclap. There was complete silence. Jim explained.

"This year's accident really upset her. She has heard all kinds of stories about the place. I have to say I'm not keen to do it again."

Without him there would be no Lotus-Ford at Indianapolis. He was talked round by Chapman. He never liked letting the side down. He overcame his fine feelings towards his family's peace of mind, and agreed. Helen Clark told an American television network. "I was very worried about it, and wasn't keen on him going at all. I was quite relieved when it was over."

Before tyres let him down in 200-lap race,
Clark races alongside Jack Brabham's John Zink-Urschel Trackburner.
Brabham lasted 77 laps, Clark 47.

Within an hour of winning one of the greatest races of his life, he was on the phone to Scotland and his mother.

The car's victory was slightly soured by a sherriff's officer detaining Chapman until a money matter was cleared up. Parnelli Jones, the bitter rival of 1963 drove for Lotus at Milwaukee and Trenton in 1964 and took Chapman to court over his pay. An error in the Lotus accounts department was blamed for the slip-up although it was difficult to see how a driver could be short-changed for so long and by such a large amount by accident.

Jim broke 19 of 20 record speeds and distances for the race; it was the first victory for a Ford engine, the first for a foreign driver for 49 years and the first for a British car with a British driver. Don Frey described the Lotus-Ford as having the greatest engine and the greatest chassis in the world which was demonstrably true. It was the result, said Frey, of a marriage between one of the world's largest and one of the world's smallest car manufacturers.

The total race prize money was $628,399 (£225,000, or £2,270,000 in 1990s money) which included lap and accessory prizes, of which the winning car took $166,621 (£60,000). Of this £28,500 was for leading for 190 of the 200 laps. American taxes accounted for $33,000. Jim took home £46,000 which would represent the best part of half a million pounds in the 1990s – still far short of what 1990s grand prix drivers were to earn. Clark won only £4,000 for an entire series of ten Tasman races of which he won nine, and £13,340 for his 1965 world championship season, perhaps his best-ever earnings. One grand prix, the French Grand Prix at Clermont Ferrand in 1965 was worth only $1,820 (£660) to him. Even taking fuel and tyre company retainers and a few advertising endorsements into account, his annual income was still well short of £100,000, something under a million in 1990s terms.

Indianapolis was among Jim Clark's most conspicuous victories. He was second again the following year when Chapman, distracted briefly from his lap chart miscounted, and Graham Hill's Lola won with Clark in second place by a whisker. Once again he had a drama at Turn Four and either through oil on the track or an uncharacteristic misjudgement spun the car through 180 degrees. He turned in the cockpit to see where he was going. The spin began at around 185mph but even as the car was slowing to 140-150mph he flicked it back through 180 degrees again and carried on. He had flat-spotted the tyres and came in to have them changed, shocking Colin Chapman and the electronic score board into losing track

of their lap chart. It was a feat never achieved at Indianapolis before, and seldom successfully since, confirming if confirmation was ever needed that Jim Clark had a spatial faculty of which an astronaut might have been proud.

Jackie Stewart had not been long in eyeing up the big money at Indy, the prize fund was up to $691,000 (£251,000) and he led from lap 147 to lap 192 until his car lost oil pressure. Never was a race seen by more people; besides 300,000 paying spectators and countless millions watching on American television it was beamed by the new wonders of satellite to audiences round the world. I watched it in a Glasgow cinema with Helen Stewart, and we squirmed in discomfort at the first lap accident involving 14 cars which had to be cleared up before the race could restart.

If everything had fallen into place, Jim Clark would have won Indianapolis an unprecedented three years in succession. He certainly helped to write Speedway history not just through his performances at the wheel, but in his special demeanour. He found winning there highly satisfactory and despite his criticisms of his rookie test (another example of how he resented criticism of his driving – even implied criticism) he enjoyed the place. He disliked facing the American barrage of publicity and accepted accolades cooly which confused the Americans. They were somewhat taken aback to find that although he was delighted, he did not express surprise at winning. "He loved it," said Beaky Sims. "He hated the hype but he loved racing at Indy. The USAC people loved him. I worked in American racing for five years, and they never forgot him."

Clark told American TV that his worries about Indy concerned other cars: "It's very difficult to say if it is more dangerous than a road course. Indianapolis is safer in that one can hit the walls, or have a glancing blow off the walls and get away with it. But when it comes to the race itself, as I've found out, you can be involved in an accident which is none of your own doing. You can run off a road course, and have a pretty nasty accident, which if there had been a wall there, as at Indy, would not have been so serious. But I think they've both got their own pros and cons. It is very difficult to say which is better."

Jim Clark, the French text assures us, "est bien le super-champion."

Stirling Moss started Clark water-skiing at East London, leaping nimbly
off the jetty behind the tow-boat.
At first attempt Jim jumped clean out of water-skis and
sank out of sight.

EXILE

J im's ill-starred local lawyer and accountant did their best to deal with his affairs, but they were out of their depth. They did the kind of thing that should have been done, but did it badly, and they were not up to dealing with the Inland Revenue. They controlled his finances completely in obedience to Jim's wishes; he simply wanted them to pay bills and send him enough money to be going on with.

Unsurprisingly they were not well received at Lotus. "Tiresome fellows," according to Andrew Ferguson. "Scottish bullocks," Chapman called them, irritated by their stream of letters designed, so far as he was concerned, to ingratiate them with their client and increase their fees. Everything was under the control of the bullocks, and was meticulously although ineffectually looked after until the losses which they suffered in the 1970s after Clark's death.

By 1962 Jim thought it better to engage his lawyer to draw up a contract for him with Lotus. He never found negotiating easy, and his lawyer had great difficulty pinning down either the wily Chapman or the street-wise Ferguson: "The bullocks' approach did nothing to soothe Colin or anyone else. They appeared unable or unwilling to accept the standard financial structures of motor racing, causing us much exasperation and frustration," wrote Ferguson. In some desperation he raised contractual issues directly with Clark, holding out the bait of, "… arranging payment as soon as he had quietened his beagles; this did little to enhance my relationship with Jimmy."

Tasman series, 1967. Lakeside, Queensland. Clark (Lotus) and Stewart (BRM).

Jim had every reason to be cautious. Ferguson's "…standard financial structures," were not serving him well, and for Indianapolis Chapman had made him pay his own expenses. In a revealing passage from *The Indianapolis Years*, Ferguson recounts how he was summoned to Chapman's office after Jim's account of the famous victory appeared in the *Daily Express*.

Sally Stokes was wary of being being photographed at races.

"'Have you seen this? he asked, jabbing the newspaper with his usual faultlessly manicured finger. I nodded.

'Oh dear, poor Jimmy!' wailed Colin. 'We spend a fortune and endless hours of work providing a winning car, and he has to spend good money paying for his underwear and socks to be laundered… my heart bleeds for him!' "

Chapman's chumminess towards his principal driver did not run deep when it came to cash. Ferguson makes no bones about his instructions, which were to obtain Clark's services cheaply and comprehensively. Might it have been any different if Clark had kept Ian Scott Watson on? Perhaps not. Chapman had made him a member of the Lotus family and it was only when Jim went for outside help that the circle was broken.

Traditionally apprehensive of smart London lawyers and accountants, but by 1966 so worried about his tax situation that he was desperate for help, on the advice of John Whitmore he went to see Peter Hetherington. A distinguished accountant with Rawlinson & Hunter which had acted for the British Racing Drivers Club since the 1930s, Hetherington was on the board of Silverstone Circuits, and an advisor to the BRDC committee. Jim saw him at his office in Green Street, close to Whitmore's London flat in Balfour Place.

It was the practice of the Inland Revenue to present apparently wealthy individuals with heavy assessments of what they thought their earnings were, and demand a large proportion of it in tax. The assessments were based on what it was thought professional sportsmen, or actors, or writers might earn, and challenged them to agree or disagree. If they agreed and simply paid up, the assessment for the following year would be larger on the grounds that if the taxpayer admitted to an estimated or assessed figure, the real one was probably larger. The cycle was repeated until the hapless taxpayer brought in an accountant who could satisfy the authorities about his real level of income and expenditure.

To someone brought up in the world of PAYE or straightforward self-employment, a notional assessment accompanied in Jim's case by a demand for £250,000 was unnerving. It was more than twice what he was earning, and he knew he had to sort things out or face severe financial penalties. Hetherington put his new client's nail-biting down to uneasiness about the meeting, but he could also see the tremendous anger Jim showed towards the Inland Revenue. His exasperation was not directed against the tax advisors who had let him down, but towards the Revenue who were facing him with excessive demands. He felt they did not realise the risks he was taking to earn his money, and said that if they thought they could carry on taking 18 shillings and threepence (91.25p) in the pound off his earnings and leave him with one and ninepence, (8.75p) they had another think coming.

He talked of the dangers of motor racing in the context of his tax assessment, and thought it unreasonable to expect this amount of tax from a man who lived with such danger. It was a nice theory, but it did not occur in tax law.

The Revenue argument was enshrined in a case known as Inland Revenue v. Errol Flynn, and they wrote to say they considered that Jim Clark was, in their word a peripatetic, like Errol Flynn. The connection lay in a tax dispute, which was a matter of record, in which Flynn contended that he had moved his domicile to California. The Revenue said no, he was always away in California or Switzerland or Monte Carlo or on a yacht or somewhere, but none of these was his proper home. He was a sort of gipsy, therefore his main home was still in England where, like other gipsies, he had to pay tax.

The Revenue found fault with a structure that Jim's accountant and lawyer had set up in the Bahamas. Some Bahamian residents had formed a company called Clarksport Ltd which employed Jim Clark to race for it. That company received all his earnings, and paid him a notional salary of £20,000 or £30,000. The difference between what he earned and what he was paid belonged to the Bahamian company, and the Revenue refused to believe that he did not have some secret agreement with it to avoid paying tax.

His new accountants went back to Jim and said they were sorry to question his integrity, but was there any agreement with Clarksport to pay him by another means? Jim said there was not, and to tell the Inland Revenue he was gambling against making one

Home at Edington Mains.
Clark fidgets.

Tasman series, 1968. Stirling Moss now retired looks on.
Clark changed to Buco helmet.

and ninepence in the pound because of them, or two shillings from his friends in Clarksport. He claimed that the odds were in his favour, and he trusted his luck with the Bahamians more than the UK Revenue.

The first assessment was sorted out, but the position was still unsatisfactory. Hetherington said it was not his business to tell people they ought to live abroad, but it was the only perfect way to save UK tax. There were some complicated schemes for avoiding UK tax, but they had flaws, and if he wanted certainty there was no alternative but to emigrate.

Jim elected to go to Bermuda on April 5, 1966. He chose it because it was half way between North America where he raced often, and Europe. The Revenue asked for the receipt from Pickfords to show that all his belongings had been removed from Edington Mains, and although it was a painful process for him, he complied with all the terms of emigration.

It was the deepest personal crisis in Jim Clark's life. Up till then the option of returning to farming had remained, and he negotiated understandings only from year to year. From then on he realised his options were limited. He had to shed his practical ties with Edington Mains and even some of his emotional ties with his family and roots. Above all he had in a sense to break away from and almost break faith with his father.

Tasman group.
Frank Gardner, Jack Brabham, Jim Clark, Ian Geoghan, Johnny Harvey, Piers Courage, and Kevin Bartlett.

"He found it an extremely painful decision," according to Peter Hetherington. "He had to sell or give away the farm that his father had given him − give it away to the family, not to an outsider. He had to remove every personal effect, all his books and papers and walking sticks and guns. He was changing domicile, and he had to show the Inland Revenue that he was severing all connections with his past."

He felt especially that he was letting his father down. His father thought that Jim one day would come back and take up the farm again, and although Jim may have told him privately that he would (perhaps with substantial sums of money behind him), it would have been ruinous to

Photographer Nigel Snowdon caught world champion working on car at
Warwick Farm, Tasman series.

hint as much to the Revenue. He may have tried to reassure his father, telling him that when he retired from racing he would return. Yet it preyed on his mind, and was the most difficult part of his decision.

It was a turning point as significant as any in his lifetime. Up till then almost every crisis could be resolved with some help from his father or acting within precepts that his father had drawn up. Like Scots law he could act on principle, not case law. Now he was on his own, forced to take advice from individuals beyond his immediate family, outside his circle of trusted acquaintances, outside Scotland even. He had relied a lot on his father's advice, but now he felt the world, in particular the world of the Inland Revenue which he blamed for forcing his hand, had dealt with him harshly.

Pinehurst, North Carolina.
Clark relaxes while racing at nearby Rockingham, October, 1967.

Jim's anger against the Revenue was of the temper he sometimes displayed in racing. There he could work out his anguish in the way he knew best, by a display of skill or bravura that had virtually no match. When it came to money, the Revenue, or intangible emotional things, he had few answers except to set them aside, put them away, bottle them up in a smouldering emotional mixture that only deepened his anxiety.

To establish that he was no longer a resident in Britain he had to show that he had not only left the UK but actually set up home somewhere else. He bought a condominium in Bermuda, at a place called Roxdene built on the site of a beautiful old Bermuda house. The rules were that he should not set foot in the United Kingdom for twelve months which meant missing some minor races. He had to show that he had minimal return to the UK in the first three years, after which he was allowed back for 90 days a year.

The Revenue claimed, unsuccessfully that Bermuda was just a pretence, that this tiny condominium was not a home, and he really spent most of his time in Paris. He denied that Paris was his home; they said his home was still Scotland. The trouble with the authorities over his money was not over yet.

Keith Duckworth, designer of Ford-Cosworth DFV
examines his brainchild, Zandvoort, 1967.

Lotus-Ford 49 1967

The arrangement between Lotus and Ford was articulated in December 1966. Jim Clark received a retainer of £5,000, but in order to tempt Graham Hill away from BRM, Ford was prepared to offer £10,000 towards the cost of his contract to Team Lotus. And just to show Ford was being even-handed it contributed a further £5,000 towards Clark's retainer, making the total £10,000.

To make sure the cash went straight to the drivers and not into the Lotus coffers, a letter was copied to them outlining what the deal was. In addition a bonus scheme was agreed guaranteeing £1,500 for a win, £1,000 for a second place, down to £100 for sixth. Colin Chapman wrote back to Ford observing that he did appreciate that these were substantial sums of money, although an essential contribution towards drivers' remunerations. He added almost wistfully: "… which is such a necessary part of the racing scene these days".

He also shrewdly included arrangements for £5,000 plus a bonus schedule to buy off Marchal and substitute Autolite.

The agreement specified, "…Sufficient engines to equip one two-car team during the 1967 season… and for as long as they remain competitive in grand prix events." Not in anybody's wildest dreams was a useful lifespan of some 23 years contemplated, with direct descendants, DFW, DFX, DFY, DFZ, DFL, and so on producing the most successful and long-lived racing engine design ever.

Chapman was apprehensive about having the eagerly-awaited DFV engine exclusively for no longer than one season. "We feel that having gone through all the heartache in the first year in sorting the engine, we should be guaranteed exclusivity and free of charge loan for two more seasons rather than suddenly finding that after having gone through all the grief, the same engine is then being offered to rival teams the following year."

He had a point. Ford was scrupulously fair but in 1968 it put its Ford-Cosworth DFV into six or seven cars at most grands prix, won 11 out of 12 of them and all three major non-title Formula 1 races. Graham Hill won his second world championship in a Lotus-Ford. In 1969 when Matra would not allow a Ford engine to run in a Matra chassis because the firm had been

Autumn, 1965 Keith Duckworth (left) and Ford's Harley Copp examine FVA, one-half of DFV.

sold to a Chrysler-controlled company Jackie Stewart was a world champion without a chassis. Tyrrell said he thought he might even get a Ferrari. Ford bought two March chassis for £24,000 and gave them to Ken Tyrrell until his own car was ready and Stewart secured the 1969 championship.

All this was still in the future when Jim Clark first saw the Lotus-Ford 49 that set the seal on his greatness. He had seen chassis jigs being made in the new Lotus works at Hethel soon after it was opened in 1966. He saw drawings, and although as a non-engineer he could not make much of them, he knew the general layout. The first engine was handed over to Chapman on April 25, 1967, two days after it was completed and five months after work started on it.

It was in the autumn of 1965 that Walter Hayes, Ford's director of public affairs, Harley Copp, director of engineering and product development, Colin Chapman and Keith Duckworth hatched the plot that would result in the DFV engine. After Ford of Europe was established in 1967, it acquired some high-grade executives from Ford of America, among whom was Copp who had commissioned the development of Ford experimental racing engines in the 1950s.

Top Detroit executives traditionally did not want to be sent abroad to the subsidiaries, because they felt it threatened their career prospects. When they got back they worried that the ranks would close, they would lose their position on the promotional ladder and in some cases it was true. People could come over, do good work and go back and find they no longer had the job they wanted. Copp was eventually made vice-president of engineering.

Hayes had overcome the difficulties over getting Ford to pay for a motor sport programme. He had initiated a rally programme and set up the competition department at Boreham without much difficulty because Sir Patrick Hennessy who had tempted him away from Fleet Street would more or less let him do what he wanted.

Henry Ford II trusted him too, but it was difficult to get Ford engineers to have anything to do with motor sport, because they did not truly regard it as their business. Harley Copp was a stroke of luck because he was the first director of engineering who had shown interest.

He was curiously iconoclastic, he hired Rolls-Royces and drove them mainly for pleasure but also to see what the opposition was like. When Hayes wanted to do the DFV, he needed some engineering respectability to persuade the accountants at Ford, and he had to talk Copp into sharing the costs on behalf of Ford engineering research. When the item came up in a Ford of Britain policy committee meeting under Any Other Business, Hayes simply put it to the assembled executives: "I would like to do a grand prix engine."

It was going to cost £100,000, not much in the great Ford scheme of things and, as has often been told to put it into perspective, only a tenth of the cost of adding synchromesh to first gear of the Cortina gearbox. Hayes also had to sell the idea to Ford in Detroit, but $323,000 compared with what Ford's whole North American competition programme was going to cost was small beer. Cosworth contracted to get £25,000 on March 1, 1966, a further staged payment of £50,000 on January 1, 1967 and the final £25,000 on January 1, 1968.

Duckworth and Mike Costin (founders with Bill Brown of Cosworth Engineering) had solid reputations as engine developers, and had evolved the successful four-cylinder FVA (Four Valve Type A) loosely based on the cylinder block of a production Ford Cortina engine. With his devastating logic, Duckworth called the V-8 DFV for Double Four Valve and Walter Hayes was worried about it. Ford had an emotional attachment to V-8 engines stemming from their advocacy of them since the 1930s, and Hayes as the real instigator of the project assured the Ford Motor Company operating policy committee headed by Henry Ford II and Benson Ford that his part of the global competition budget of $1,683,500 (£610,000 – £6,000,000 in 1990s value) was being wisely spent.

"I told Henry Ford quite simply that this car was going to win grand prix races, and I laid down the law in a letter to Chapman in September 1966. I told him that I know what it's going to do but I don't want anybody else to know what it's going to do, and therefore I don't want you to make any press announcements or talk to anybody about it."

Duckworth had never designed a complete engine before, yet it was a measure of the success he had achieved with the FVA that Ford kept its word on the development of the DFV for the Lotus 49. There were only three factors in Walter Hayes's mind. Two were practical and commercial. One was emotional. The first was to put Ford in the forefront of

Jackie Stewart, still struggling with H-16 BRM enviously eyes DFV with Chapman, Lotus designer Maurice Philippe, and Graham Hill.

grand prix motor racing, the second was to provide a British engine to keep Lotus in the forefront of grand prix motor racing.

The third and perhaps the most compelling was to make Jim Clark once again world champion.

Yet some of the pundits had doubts about the adequacy of eight cylinders for the new 3.0-litre Formula 1. Twelve looked like being the absolute minimum and BRM were going ahead with 16. Hayes: "Everybody was going to laugh me to scorn about it being a V-8. Indeed when we showed it in Ford's little showroom in Regent Street, there were some giggles about it being a V-8."

Hayes's programme of restraining expectations for the new engine got under way with his letter to Chapman, "There will be no publicity about the car or engine up to the point of its first Grand Prix event ... The press at the moment have no idea of the fine progress that Keith (Duckworth) has made and I think you will agree that it is sensible to keep both car and engine under wraps until we can all obtain maximum impact."

Clark was not able to take part in any testing before the first car was completed during May 1967 owing to his self-imposed exile. The first time he saw the completed car was when it was unloaded from the transporter at Zandvoort. The basis of the car was not unfamiliar to him, for it was an evolution of Chapman's Lotus 43, the abbreviated monocoque designed for the stop-gap, complicated, overweight but cleverly conceived BRM H-16 engine of 1966 which Clark took to its only grand prix win in America.

The 43 had been the first Lotus in which the engine was designed to form a stressed part of the car. The 49 with the Ford-Cosworth DFV was the second; slimmer and smaller than the 43, made of 18swg aluminium sheet, it was in effect a bathtub holding the driver and 40 gallons of fuel, with the engine bolted firmly to the rear. At the front of the bathtub was a bulkhead subframe carrying the pedals, the oil and water radiators, and the front suspension. Everything at the back, the wheels, gearbox, final drive and suspension hung on the engine block. In conception it was magnificent, in execution it was elegant, and in accomplishment it was sublime.

Yet there seemed no point in expecting it to win. Getting two cars to the start line was achievement enough.

Clark's initial reaction was guardedly optimistic. The engine had a great deal of power but it was not evenly distributed throughout the engine speed range. "You think you've only got one engine, then all of a sudden you start going and you find you've got another engine as well." He had not done any testing, but nobody else had done much either. Long weeks of pre-race testing for grand prix drivers or even substitute up-and-coming test drivers still lay well into the future.

There was not much time to make changes to suit Clark when the two cars reached Zandvoort. Graham Hill had already driven chassis number 49/1 so it was effectively race-ready. Clark climbed into 49/2 with the spring-rates and damper settings Hill preferred. He had not even been able to go to the factory to have a seat fitting although he did feel that this should not have been necessary. "It was a matter of packing and padding and setting the pedals and steering wheel," he said. "After all these years, Lotus had a pretty good idea of my shape."

On the second day of practice a hub ball-race in a rear wheel broke up and Clark, apprehensive about reliability, refused to drive the car again until the problem was put right. His horror of mechanical failures was growing to a point where he was becoming quite difficult with the team. It was not without cause. After eight years he had seen every sort of accident happen, and was very taut.

He did not altogether trust new cars. Only the previous year Lotus had tried to get him into a car that was too small for him, an occasion he spoke of with great indignation. "I got back from testing at Indianapolis and tried out the Formula 1 and Formula 2 cars and found I couldn't even get into the damn things. I was sitting with one hip higher than the other." Lotus had built the cars an inch narrower in its effort to reduce frontal area but they no longer fitted the driver. Hollows had to be beaten out in every car's cockpit to accommodate the Clark buttocks. He had not put on weight. "They just thought, 'He drove the bloody thing last year and he seemed to have plenty of room, if he didn't complain he must have had too much, so we'll make it an inch narrower'."

There was no such trouble with the 49 because it had to be big enough for Graham Hill. Clark tried the firmer Hill springing on the 49 at Zandvoort and typically could not make up his mind which he preferred. "Actually I don't know," he said after practice. "I like Graham's springs that I had on yesterday, I think they were probably better than the ones I've got on now, but I want to

Graham Hill's mind focused resolutely on racing. Famously relaxed away from track; unapproachable in cockpit.

try softer ones, go back to my own settings. I've put them back on for today and the car feels all right, but I think it was probably just as good on Graham's settings."

Clark's first impressions of the 49, except for the hiatus over the rear hub ball-race were of approval. It seemed quick, but he was startled by the way the engine power came in, his 'two engines'. "You want to be able to drive occasionally at lowish rpm and pull away with a lot of torque. The DFV doesn't have this at all. When the power comes in at 6,500rpm it does so with such a bang that the car is almost uncontrollable. You either have power or you haven't. The throttle control is a bit basic, very stiff with no decent travel. It feels a bit odd with only a wire cable and the throttle responses are not good at all."

This was not the routine Jim Clark, loyal, trusting, acquiescent. He was looking for an even response all the way up the rev range and he no longer minded saying what he thought. There was very little power below 6,500rpm, at which point it came in so abruptly that it led to wheelspin. The sudden loss of grip in a corner, "… especially if you're in a bit of an attitude", (a Clark euphemism for sliding the car in a controlled way through a bend) was potentially dangerous. At Zandvoort coming on to the straight where the track was oily, when the engine reached 6,500rpm in fourth gear the back wheels began to over-speed and the car was squirming down the track with the tail wagging from side to side. "It was quite alarming, I was going down the straight swinging the steering from one side to the other trying to keep the car on the road."

The brake ratio was uneven but was cured by different pads. The wrong pad material had been used and the braking at the front was deficient. The clutch did not work very well either, yet the car felt solid, and handled well for its first outing.

The race on the sand-dunes by the coast swept by the same winds that blew over Edington Mains 400 miles away across the grey North Sea is enshrined in motor sporting folklore. Hill led from the start, Clark followed from the third row of the grid until Hill's car coasted into the pits with broken teeth in the timing gear. Clark took the lead and won an exhilarating victory. "I would never have thought it possible," he said. "When I drove the car first, apart from the trouble with a rear hub, I felt we could do very well. I probably still had faith in Colin. I had a lot of faith in Keith Duckworth too, and felt that between them they could achieve a winning car. I worked with Keith's engines for a long time in Formula Junior and gained great respect for him. I felt sure the engine had a chance

Alan Fearnley's pilot sketch for his Zandvoort painting.

of finishing. Zandvoort is not hard on the gearbox and clutch, so I thought they would stand up. After that it was down to me."

Hayes and Keith Duckworth could scarcely believe their good fortune. Clark won by half a minute. A Lotus 49 was on pole position for the next 11 grands prix; the car was a year ahead of all the opposition. Not since the days of Mercedes-Benz had a grand prix motor racing team shown such overwhelming dominance. It hardly mattered that mechanical frailties and a certain amount of bad management robbed it of a string of successes throughout the rest of the season, or so it might have seemed to any other team or any other driver.

It mattered to Jim Clark.

Franco Lini photographed David Phipps 6ft 2in, Jim Clark 5ft 7¼in at Zandvoort.

Ford and Lotus scored such moral superiority in 1967 that they went down in motor racing folklore at the expense of Brabham-Repco which took the constructors' championship, and Denny Hulme who won the drivers'. Winning first time out for a new engine and car was almost unknown in the history of grand prix racing; it would have been too much to expect the rest of the season to pass without incident.

The disasters, so far as Jim Clark was concerned, began with the very next race, the Belgian Grand Prix at Spa, when Hill retired with transmission trouble and Clark was lucky to finish sixth after plug trouble. Both cars went out in the French Grand Prix and the situation was only retrieved in the British when Clark won. Hill suffered suspension troubles in both practice and the race. By the German Grand Prix morale was slipping and Jim Clark's patience was wearing thin.

He talked cheerfully enough to David Phipps, a leading motor racing photo-journalist, on the record about the car and the season's racing. "The Lotus 49 has twice the horse power of the Formula 1 cars I have driven before or in fact any single seater apart from the Indianapolis cars which are very different, very high geared and never drop much below 140mph. They say we should not let the revs drop below 6,500rpm, but it is sometimes difficult to avoid. Life can be a bit hectic when you are coming out of a corner and it suddenly hits on all eight cylinders."

Did he feel the chassis was as good as previous Lotuses? "It's impossible to separate the chassis from the engine and the tyres ... It feels as if the car gets up on its back wheels as you turn into a corner and the

Heat-haze at Spa, 1967.
Interminable Masta Straight shimmers as Clark's Lotus 49 approaches at 185mph.

Silverstone triumph.
Michael Cooper catches
Clark almost brushing the
breeze-blocks on
inside of corner.

back end tends to flick out very suddenly … The fixed ratio gearbox has been frustrating…"

Significantly Clark responded to Phipps's questions about the apparent change that had taken place in his approach to racing. When it was put to him that he no longer seemed to go for a quick lead in a race and demoralise the opposition, he said: "I have been conscious of the fact that the car is new and a little brittle so I've been quite happy just to be in the lead. I have always felt that the car would go quickly if it was really necessary and it certainly proved this at Monza, but I have preferred to nurse it as much as possible. I am probably still a little suspicious of it. I can't say that I expect anything in particular to fall off, but I'm not a hundred per cent happy with the handling and I'm always a little doubtful about the brakes."

What a contrast with the solid confidence he had in Chapman and his cars in earlier years.

Jackie Stewart saw the difference in Clark by 1967: "Jimmy was no longer the Border farmer depending on Colin. I saw the change. He was a different man. He was more independent, more vocal about what he wanted. I thought Colin was going to have more and more trouble with him."

By the German Grand Prix at the Nürburgring in August, Clark's mood had changed even more. There was disillusionment in an off-the-record yet tape-recorded interview he gave in private.

Following the success at Zandvoort he was disappointed not to win at Spa. "I never anticipate winning. But I reckoned we had a fair chance there, and it was really very comfortable while the car was going. There was no problem. I never had to go really hard. I was more disappointed than anything that the second pit stop took place because after the first one, even though I might not have been in a position to win. I was all set to have a real old go. We could have seen some amazing lap times because although the practice times would not have stood up in the race, we could have gone round Spa very quickly. But if we were going to have a go in the race it was going to be after the first pit stop and then we never got another full lap without the plugs falling out. After that the gears all went."

He had been preparing for a great charge from the back like the one he would make at Monza at the end of the season. He was ready to apply the same self-induced stress that produced such astonishing performances at Germany in 1962 and Monaco in 1964.

There was talk at the time that one of the spark plugs unscrewed itself because of vibration from the engine, but Jim crossly said: "The porcelain

broke. It blew right out of one plug and broke in half in the other one. I think they were over-tightened."

Chapman had not wanted anything to do with Autolite spark plugs, the preferred Ford brand. Chapman wrote to Ford: "We have a very great problem … We are already committed by a long-term agreement to use Marchal spark plugs and this has two more years to run, namely 1967 and 1968. I must ask to be released from the insistence on Autolite spark plugs."

Ford replied: "The engines will employ Autolite spark plugs. There will be no arrangement with any other plug manufacturer. Should you encounter any problems Harley Copp will arrange for an Autolite engineer to handle it." In due course they did and the engine ran happily on Autolite from then on.

The French Grand Prix was run at Le Mans on the Bugatti circuit which should have suited the Lotus 49. "It was our sort of circuit where you've got to stop and drag-race away from corners, These cars were going to be good at that, with lots of power for their weight. We could have out-accelerated the opposition from the corners even though we could not make much use of the great power we had in the corners. The car was still too twitchy. You could not get the power on through the middle of a corner. You had to leave it a bit later. I suppose it was something to do with it being 3.0 litres, and we weren't used to it", Clark recalled.

The power of the 3.0-litre cars needed to be treated with respect. "The Lotus 49 has probably more power in relation to its weight than any pure road-racing car ever, so naturally it's going to take a bit of getting used to. With that amount of power and the light weight things happen bloody quickly."

The comparison with the Indianapolis cars' power was valid, but Jim explained how it was not quite the same as a Formula 1 car. "An Indy car is geared for 200mph, and you run between 7,000 and 9,000rpm on one high gear ratio. The pulling power transmitted to the wheels in gearing of that sort is not really great. In comparison to a grand prix car in second or third or fourth gear, or even fifth with a low ratio final drive, sticking your boot on the throttle produces a quite different effect, especially when it comes in with a bang at 6,500rpm half-way round a corner as the 49 does. It is much more exciting and takes a lot more watching. At Indy you may be going faster but things happen more slowly. The power comes in gradually. It's there all the time."

The British Grand Prix had been a sweet victory: "I always like to win

Acknowledging the applause, Silverstone 1967
with Keith Duckworth behind smiling and
RAC's Dean Delamont on right.

in front of a British crowd, especially the biggest race of the year, so naturally I was very happy. Also it was the last chance in the first half of the season to get some points to try and stay in the hunt for the championship. Otherwise I think we would have been without hope, because of the way they've split the championship this year. I reckon we're still in with a fighting chance even with five races to go, although we can only count four of them. We didn't do very well in the first six races, we only scored in three, so we've got to try and do better."

By then he was either growing accustomed to the 49, or changes to the linkage aimed at giving progressive throttle response were so successful that the car was easier to drive. Modifications to the springing made it more refined, but, he warned, "… it's still not perfect".

Even after a good practice lap at the Nürburgring, it was significant that Clark still did not think he was getting the best out of the 49. "I don't think I've got the maximum out of the car," he admitted. "Its potential is much greater than I'm prepared to drive it at the moment. I reckon that I should be able to open the throttle more than I'm doing in certain instances. That's what it boils down to. I should be going quicker out of corners."

His Friday morning lap time was 8min 43.4sec, fifth fastest; Graham Hill did 8min 31.7sec in the second session in which Clark improved to 8min 19.8sec still only seventh fastest. By Saturday Clark had gone round in 8min 04.1sec, nearly 10sec better than anybody else. Next fastest was Denny Hulme (Brabham-Repco) with 8min 13.5sec, Jackie Stewart (BRM H-16) 8min 15.2sec, and Dan Gurney (Eagle-Weslake) 8min 16.9sec. He was still far from satisfied. He was convinced it was possible to get round in under 8 minutes. "I'm sure of it. On that lap I had a lot of brake trouble. It was on my second or third lap with these pads on the back and I think they were still fading, and I was also getting knock-off which was not very reassuring. I thought it was all fade and I was being a bit cautious on the brakes because of that. But you know I've only had two laps at speed in the two days' practice and I reckon I knocked four seconds off between the first and the second. I think with more experimenting of gear changes I could go on taking four seconds a lap off. The trouble is that a lot of the time I'm down in the 5,500 to 6,000 rev band where there's nothing, no power. It's a choice between keeping in a lower gear and using a bit more power, but that makes it so difficult to control that you tend to leave it in a higher gear instead."

Clark compared the transition from the less powerful 1.5-litre Lotus

25 to the 3.0-litre 49, and how it stretched him. "It was easier to get the maximum out of the Lotus 25 or 33 than it is to get a maximum out of this. It's easier to get the maximum out of a Formula 2 car round the Nürburgring than it is out of the 3.0-litre. It must be. I think it is more difficult for me, because unless I have to I won't bother. It's not so much being lazy, it's just that you're nursing the thing; you're worried something's going to break. This is one of the big worries around the 'Ring. You could drive the car much harder at times, but you're graunching along the track surface in places so hard that you just don't feel like doing it all the time. Almost every lap round here you keep thinking there's something falling off. You hit a bump differently or something happens, or your shock absorbers are getting weak – they're getting clapped out. You start pattering across the road, and you immediately think there's something coming off the car. It's still difficult to tell round here because it is so rough and bumpy, so when there is something wrong you're completely on edge wondering what it could be, having a look to see if there's anything, and all this is costing you time because you're not concentrating on your driving."

During Saturday's practice Graham Hill misjudged his braking on the fast descent to Adenau Bridge and crashed heavily, wrecking Lotus-Ford 49/3 and escaping without injury. Clark was growing more restive with every such incident. Did it make him stop and think?

"Not half it does. It certainly did. I went past Graham on a flying lap and all the rest of the way down that hill to Adenau I began to go round everything on the car wondering what broke, or if something broke why did he go off. Obviously it's going to affect you, until you know what it was."

I was with Jim Clark that day. Lotus had a room at the Sporthotel behind the main grandstand at the Nürburging and we spent a good deal of the afternoon and evening watching him making headway with a girl working on a film crew. My wife had introduced them and we were all anxious to know what the outcome of the encounter would be.

I don't think we ever did. Jim was his customary guarded self. But his demeanour suggested that his approach to motor racing had indeed shifted. We put it down to Hill's accident. It was put to Jim that he had been fortunate to emerge unscathed from his years at Lotus even after accidents to other drivers. His response to questions of this sort was often bland, sometimes light-hearted; usually he deflected them altogether. Like Jabby Crombac, I knew there were areas it was unproductive to mention.

Graham Hill struggles
with Watkins Glen trophy,
Jim gave bowl to
Walter Hayes.
Duckworth and Chapman
contemplate success.
US Grand Prix, 1967.

America was happy hunting ground; two wins at Watkins Glen,
a win and two second places at Indianapolis, victory at Milwaukee,
first and second at Riverside Grand Prix.

Sometimes he simply would not answer at all. His self-control was usually perfect. On this occasion we ventured into tricky territory and Jim went straight into high gear, recalling in particular Zandvoort, when he warned the team that there was something wrong with the rear hub during practice, and he was not going to drive the car until it was put right.

Question: "It appears that you've been jolly lucky in this respect haven't you, even now and in the past to the detriment or misfortune of other drivers. You've always come out just a little bit on top haven't you?"

Jim: "Nothing broke on Graham's car today. He had something break at Silverstone, I had something break at Zandvoort. What is it? You say luck. At Zandvoort I could have gone on until that bloody wheel fell off, but the night before I told them there was something wrong with the car but they didn't find it. The next day I was sure there was something wrong with the car and I just brought it in and I just wouldn't bloody well drive it until they'd found it. They found it all right. You could hardly see it but it was there. It's a very difficult conflict with your own conscience to make sure that you're getting it right. There's a difference between thinking there's something wrong but you don't want to be an old woman about it, or being sensible and saying I'm convinced there's something wrong, you've got to find it. I'm not taking sides against anybody or anything, but this has happened in the past several times. Then you think thank God I took that decision."

Dave (Beaky) Sims, the Lotus mechanic, found Clark's technical knowledge ample. "He could interpret what the car was doing. He might say that the front end was 'washing out', needed more grip, and then he'd say how best to do it. His technical ability and feel for what the car was doing was phenomenal. It was uncanny. Unique. He knew when something was wrong. He'd feel a slight vibration in the rear and we'd pull the car about and find nothing. He'd insist something was still amiss and later we'd discover a wheel bearing was going."

Yet the dichotomy was asserting itself. His obsession with racing was keeping him in it but he was being crushed with anxiety about the likelihood of a serious accident over which he increasingly felt he had no control. The command, for which he felt such a deep need was now beyond him, yet he still enjoyed the idea of motor racing. He was asked if he missed sports cars and saloon car racing and whether he was taking advantage of the extra time he had to spare in exile. "I think I'm enjoying not being quite so busy. But at times, when I see saloon car racing I feel like … I wish … I feel like having a go."

Clark was delighted with Ford-Cosworth DFV even though,
"It was two engines really…"

He talked almost wistfully about the old days with Andrew Russell, and Rest-and-be-Thankful, and Border Rallies long gone, and the palmy days of the Scottish Rally when he drove for the fun of it. American television was calling him the most famous Scotsman since Robert Burns but eight years of Formula 1 motor racing had left him emotionally drained; the greatest driver in history after Fangio, he may have been outwardly at peace, but inwardly he was in turmoil.

Clark's technical awareness had reached a point where he was scrutinising every aspect of a car's behaviour, with his superb sensitivity searching for problems. Remember Stewart's analysis that he was perpetually looking for trouble even when it was not there. Now he scrutinised his whole philosophy, and yet almost to the end never betrayed the inner misgivings and apprehensions that were depleting his strength and his confidence.

The remainder of the season was a see-saw affair with the highlight of Monza and the dramatic finish at Watkins Glen when with a clear lead over Graham Hill's Lotus a bolt in Clark's rear suspension broke two laps from the end. True to form he won, but with the rear wheel leaning inwards at an odd angle. It was not enough to take the world championship however, which went to Denny Hulme driving the Brabham-Repco.

For 1968 Lotus-Ford was relaunched with cigarette sponsorship. Clark won first race of big-money era of motor racing.

Watkins Glen was a vital race for Walter Hayes whose reputation was riding on it: "I really wanted to do well in the American Grand Prix. I said to Jimmy and to Graham. 'This is the first race that this car's going to have in the United States on the home ground of Ford Motor Company, who have given me their blessing for this venture, and set the seal on all the other things we'd done in motor sport. And we're not going to screw around, we're going to go and get it right.' We did a lot more testing before we got to the United States Grand Prix and then these two asses started competing with one another in practice, and I had to make them toss up as to which of them was going to win. Then Jimmy won and gave me the trophy, and I put it on my knees in the helicopter and carried it all the way home, and really thought this was a great thing. We all felt that it was, there seemed no question that there was a great and glorious future ahead of us. "

"And then we had a terrible year didn't we?"

Clark as fans knew him; keen eyed, handsome,
winner all the way.

EPILOGUE

Jim Clark trusted his family completely and they never failed him. He would have been 60 in March 1996 and their loyalty was as unwavering then as it was when he was 30. Andrew Russell, Billy Potts and Eric Bryce, his farm steward, were all staunchly loyal; Ian Scott Watson, Jock McBain, the Somervails, Ossie Brewis and many more of his close associates had been just as steadfast.

The Borders were his anchor. He loved the region and the people he was really closest to lived there, even in the twilight of his life. Jim's emigration, although it may have been prompted by the Inland Revenue, when it occurred was more complete than he perhaps realised. The question was, would he really have picked up the traces again if, as it seemed, he was contemplating retiring from motor racing?

The wrangling with the authorities about money did not cease even on his death. The Scottish Estate Duty Office tried to suggest that a man of such world repute and success would not live in a little condominium in Bermuda. Estate duty was due on his money in Britain. It was shown to them that a similar apartment had been good enough for a former British ambassador to Washington, and a chairman of ICI, so it was probably good enough for Jim Clark.

The argument dragged on for eight years. The authorities counted the number of days he had spent at Roxdene in the two years before his death, and although it was probably only three or four weeks, it was demonstrable by examining the racing calendar precisely when he had been in Europe for the grand prix season, Australia and New Zealand for the Tasman Series, and when a gap did occur he had gone back to Bermuda.

The Estate Duty Office even argued that anybody who changed his domicile would be expected to be buried in the place they were claiming was their future home. They had to be persuaded that whatever Jim Clark might have wished, it was impossible to stop someone moving his body somewhere else. His intention might have been to be buried in Bermuda. It was on the advice of accountants that his headstone says "of Duns and Bermuda".

Such was the tangled web round the life of Jim Clark because he had this arcane proficiency in driving.

Six years after he died, his lawyer and accountant delivered a shock to his friends and family. Almost all Jim's money had been lost in an imprudent investment. The pair had been advisers to both Jim and Ian Scott Watson. They probably had no intention to cheat, but they had to stand trial for their misdemeanours one pleading guilty, one not, and both receiving prison sentences.

The lawyer was deputy sheriff of Berwickshire and the county's leading legal personage, apparently beyond reproach, which made the event so incredible when it happened. The accountant had accommodation in the same office, and was probably even more aware of the probity of what he was doing. The money had been put into an investment in America, but because it was strictly against exchange control regulations and was due back within a short time it was a high-risk strategy.

The difficulties dragged on, the money never came back and Ian Scott Watson realised there was something seriously amiss. He returned early from a holiday and the matter was reported at once to the Law Society. Jim's mistake was less a matter of naïvity than simply trusting people because they were Scottish. Crombac said: "Jim was so Scots he believed a Scotsman could never fleece him".

Within days of Clark's death Adrian Ball, a public relations consultant who handled Jim's affairs, rang David Benson with a proposition to write a book about him. Benson angrily told him that he had an agreement that Jim would sign every page of any manuscript they wrote together, and he would do a book only if Ball could still arrange that. I turned Ball down as well.

One reason for Benson's anger with Ball was the story, which may be apocryphal, that he had been to blame for Jim's difficulties with the Inland Revenue. He was reported as having aggravated Jim's tax situation by boasting in a West End restaurant how cleverly he and Jim's accountant were outwitting the inspectors of taxes, and detailing how Jim's winnings at Indianapolis were to be dealt with. A senior official of the Inland Revenue was sitting at the next table, and the result was the heavy tax assessment which led to Jim's approach to a new accountant and his subsequent emigration.

There was a newspaper story that half his Indianapolis winnings were being held back in the United States while his tax position was sorted out, which Clark found intensely embarrassing. When they saw each other for the last time in Barcelona just before he died Jim told Benson: "We can talk about anything except tax."

Jim by then was entirely in the hands of his advisors, and his overseas earnings were quite legitimately being invested off-shore. It was the view of almost everybody who ever did business with Jim Clark that he would never do anything dishonest, and never try to evade tax.

By 1967 Jim Clark had become quite outgoing, although traces did remain of the shy, unpretentious Border farmer. Twice world champion, widely acclaimed as a great sporting driver and recognised everywhere, he was awarded an OBE in June 1964. He was feted and adored by the famous, and was on a transatlantic shuttle between Paris and qualifying days at Indianapolis. But he was also due to take part in a Formula 2 race at Pau and it was touch and go whether he would make it in time for Friday practice, since he was due back at Orly from the United States that morning. The timing was tight.

His Piper Twin Comanche was fuelled up and standing by at the small airport at Toussus-le-Noble. He asked customs officials if he could please be cleared quickly, and went over the route from Orly, making pace notes so that he knew every corner. The plan was to drive there without delay, and fly himself to Pau.

He discussed the best way of transferring from the Indianapolis flight to the transatlantic terminal at Kennedy Airport, New York, with Jackie Stewart who said, "Easy. Go to the VIP club. A special car will take you right across the airport." Jim shook his head. "The VIP club? I could never do that."

He made the transfer on his own, with his luggage, and got to Pau on time. He would never pull rank on an unsuspecting airline servant, although he would berate a Galaxie driver at Crystal Palace who promised, and then failed, to let him out first for practice in the Lotus Cortina.

His approach to the RAC Rally which he so enjoyed in 1966 was deadly serious. He took part in a Ford Lotus-Cortina with Brian Melia, an experienced co-driver. Graham Hill competed in a Mini-Cooper with David Benson, and when journalists descended on them early in the rally Bill Barnet, Ford's rally competition manager, could not help noticing the difference between them. Hill told the press it was all a bit of a giggle really, while Jim provided them with a careful analysis of rally driving. His systematic tactics were reflected in his stage times.

The regular rally drivers were sceptical, believing Ford, BMC, and the two grand prix drivers were only engaged for

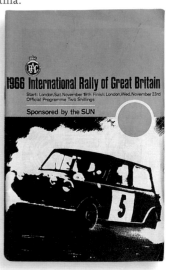

RAC Rally.
By Scotland the damage
was done, yet Clark's drive
ranks with 1967 Monza as
testimony to genius.
In Aberfoyle
Michael Turner's painting
shows Ford team under
Stuart Turner (glasses behind
car) assesses damage for
Clark and co-driver
Brian Melia.

publicity. Yet Clark was more competitive than anybody had thought possible. He was seldom out of the top 10; he was fastest on three stages, second fastest on seven, third on four and fourth on five. On the 40th, in Loch Achray, he crashed, inflicting severe damage on the Lotus Cortina. He then rolled into a ditch on the 45th, Glengap. "We tripped over the Border," he said, and so they had.

The hitherto almost invincible Swedish drivers were generous in their praise. In the course of the one event Clark had progressed from being unexpectedly quick to being a potential winner. The speed with which he advanced was further proof of the mastery he could bring to any driving task. He demonstrated mastery within hours of techniques experienced rally drivers had taken years to perfect. He eventually tore the side out of the car at Aberfoyle and overturned in the south of Scotland but by then it did not matter. He had shown his proficiency at car-driving; the gyros could spin just as accurately in a rally car as a racing car.

Typically he told journalists that first night: "Brian should have been driving on these stages, he's far quicker than I am. But I'm getting used to it". They loved him for that, and he meant it. He amiably disparaged Graham Hill: "He's playing at it. What does he mean coming on the RAC Rally in a works Mini Cooper, and bringing a bloody journalist?" It was his friend David Benson.

By 1966 Clark was learning how to handle the press. He had been watching Hill's breezy manner and here was a chance to match it. He did not think Hill was competing seriously and was indeed only doing it for publicity, not to mention the money the organisers and sponsors were paying him to generate media interest.

They were also paying Jim Clark, but that was a secondary consideration. The professional co-driver with him reflected how earnestly he took it however, and also how Ford took it. His attitude to his rivals was along the lines of: "We'll show these Swedish buggers…" British rally drivers of the day were seldom so competitive against Scandinavians.

He also showed his love of the sport and his generosity towards individuals when his car was declared unfit for further combat. He joined the service crew in another Lotus Cortina and carried on round the route. They had never known such enthusiasm from any driver, far less a double world champion and Indianapolis winner. There was no question of desertion just because his car was out of the rally. He saw it through. There was not one member of the entire Ford competitions staff, the service crews, and even his rival drivers who did not become staunch, faithful, and lifetime devotees of Jim Clark. They would have followed him to the ends of the earth.

Bill Barnet said Ford paid Clark £3,000, some of which he blew on treating the entire team to dinner at the Master Robert Motel near London Airport. Barnet was astonished at how little conceit or vanity there was about Jim. Some of Jim's friends who regarded him as a bit of a tight-wad would have been surprised at his beneficence.

Walter Hayes had not particularly wanted Jim to take part because he did not think that he would have anything to prove and there was no point in not doing well: "It was a sparkling performance of course. And I knew it would be a sparkling performance, but you can't always cross barriers in motor sport. Stirling Moss was the only other driver I know who was marvellous in all types of cars."

An earlier generation had been affected by the 84 deaths in the Le Mans disaster of 1955 as too high a price to pay in the name of sport, and the reforms that followed were far-reaching. Jim Clark's death touched people who up till then had believed that danger on the track could be outmanoeuvred, if only a driver had the skill.

In Jim Clark they had a driver with the most skill in the world.

The danger of motor racing was self-evident, but he had spun at astonishing speeds at Indianapolis and achieved the impossible. When his car seemed out of control he could always get it back, and except for rare lapses, an accident seemed out of the question. His injury or death was so unthinkable that some people had simply never thought about it.

The Hon Patrick Lindsay talks ERA with Clark at Rouen, 1964.

When the unthinkable happened, as at Le Mans thirteen years before, the price seemed too high in the name of a sport, and things had to change.

In due course they did. Jim Clark's death altered the climate to one in which the reforming zeal of Jackie Stewart and his great driver safety crusade of the 1970s flourished. The accidents of Scarfiotti, Spence, Rindt, and Pedro Rodriguez who shared the grid of Clark's final Grand Prix quickened the pace of reform, yet it was the certainty that even the greatest driver of all was vulnerable that ensured the changes would be accepted.

Joy of driving. Crombac and Clark with Pierre Bardinon's Bugatti 35B.

Clark's chroniclers underrated his personal charm, and over-played his shyness. Jim could shed his reticence quickly if he wanted to, and he enjoyed the recognition he achieved, although he was careful not to show it. His curiosity weaned on the Ford tractors of Edington Mains and the venerable Alvis Speed Twenty led him to a prodigious variety of driving.

The Hon Patrick Lindsay was impressed when Jim drove his ERA 'Remus' in 1964 at Rouen. Fourteen members of the Vintage Sports Car Club (VSCC) took their cars across the Channel for a ten-lap race on the grand prix circuit. Lindsay was fastest in practice and offered to let Clark drive it. He took the upright, elderly car on to the track after instruction from ERA expert Douglas Hull on its pre-selector gearbox. He had never driven anything like it. Within four laps he astonished everybody by being not only faster than its owner, but driving it faster than any ERA had been driven before. He came back making suggestions about how it could be changed to make it even faster.

In September 1967 he drove his Ford Galaxie with Jabby Crombac to wine-grower Pierre Bardinon's newly created private circuit at Mas du Clos near Aubusson. Here he drove several of Bardinon's fine collection of cars, including a D-type Jaguar, and an assortment ranging from a Type 51 Bugatti to an ex-Fillipinetti 412 P3/P4 Ferrari with Crombac as passenger. "I was often driven by Jimmy and got no impression of speed because he drove so smoothly. I told him it was kind of him not to go fast and frighten me. Then Pierre told us we had set a new lap record at 1min 30sec."

To car-enthusiast Crombac's frustration, Bardinon and Clark talked farming. Bardinon said life in Creuse resembled Jim's in Scotland and together they enjoyed sampling some of the wines in Bardinon's extensive cellars. "Jimmy enjoyed French food accompanied by a good Bordeaux. He liked to talk about wine, in fact he shared my passion for wine."

What a sophisticate he had become.

Clark raced the Felday-4 BRM 56 four-wheel-drive car in the 1966 Brands Hatch Guards Trophy, winning the class and making fastest lap before being black-flagged for oil smoke.

His exploits in Ford Lotus Cortinas endeared him to a racing public well beyond the realms of Formula 1. Colin Chapman's first designs for the Lotus Cortina were not an unqualified success. Len Terry, the designer was taken round the factory when he joined Lotus and when he saw the Lotus-Cortina warned Chapman that the live rear axle, which resembled one he had designed for his Terrier racing car, would lead to oversteer, or tail-heaviness, and the inside rear wheel would leave the ground on corners.

Terry was proved right when Jim Clark tested a car at Snetterton, so Chapman told him to redesign it. He did, and the Lotus Cortina developed understeer instead. Clark became the darling of the trackside photographers with the inside front wheel 9 inches clear of the track. He loved showing off in a Lotus Cortina.

Would Jim Clark have gone back to the farm when he stopped?

"Everybody asks that," says Jabby Crombac. "It would have remained his base. He would have had somebody run it for him. But he would have probably found a job in the PR side of motor racing. He could not have stopped travelling the world. He had got the taste for it."

There was a chance that he might have gone into the aviation business with Colin Chapman. They were both fascinated by flying and Chapman was working on designs for a Lotus aircraft. He wanted to start with microlights and work his way up, and Clark would have been a likely partner.

Ian Scott Watson thought Jim would have wanted to have retained his home and his connections in Scotland, but not be tied to running the farm. He could have got a manager to help and kept a strong interest in it, but not have been involved in the day to day matters.

Joy of driving. Felday four-wheel-drive sports car in Guards Trophy at Brands Hatch.

Sally agreed: "I would have thought he would have gone back. Who can tell? I could never quite see Jimmy developing a career like Jackie, I wouldn't have thought that he could have lived in Monaco or Bermuda or somewhere like that once he'd finished."

She spoke on the telephone with Jimmy shortly before the accident. "He was talking about retiring and I can't remember what prompted it, but it was something like, 'Well, what if I died?

Joy of driving. Top, before driving Bardinon's
Ecurie Filipinetti Ferrari. Below, after.

What if I got killed on the track?' I was so surprised
and so jolted, because he'd never mentioned it before
in all the years I knew him. I wondered if he actually
thought about it and was considering retiring."

Jackie Stewart felt that there might have been
something at the back of Clark's mind that was going
to take him back to Edington Mains, but he did not
think Clark would have entertained a career in motor
racing. "He would never have had a team. *He would never
have had a team.* He would have gone back to Chirnside.
To Edington. To Duns. He'd have made enough money
that enabled him to do other things maybe, but his
central activity would have been there. I don't know
what he would have done in motor racing. He was so
uncomfortable. Colin Chapman did everything for
him, and in Paris Jabby helped him do anything.
Anybody he did business with would tell you he never
wanted to make decisions. He would always put you
off, 'Well I'll think about it, and I'll let you know.' His
whole life was like that."

Peter Hetherington thought he would not have
gone back, at least not so long as his father was alive.
His horizons had been broadened so much. "He was
leading a sort of Jeckyl and Hyde existence and he felt badly about it when
he went back. He felt guilty about the kind of international life he was
leading, but he could have gone back to it had he decided to retire."

Might he have found some niche in motor racing after he had
retired? Probably not. When he had worked out who he was, he would
have made up his mind what to do. My inclination is to believe with Jackie
that he would have gone back to the farm, because I do not think he had
the qualities that enabled Stewart to create Stewart Ford Grand Prix, or
James Hunt, Jonathan Palmer or John Watson to discover a role as a TV
commentator.

He was unlikely to have been a team manager. He could not have
been anybody's great corporate representative because although he would
make speeches if you forced him, they were seldom the sort of speeches
that companies or sponsors would want to hear.

Walter Hayes could have done what he did with Jackie Stewart and
pressed him into service with Ford Motor Company, as a consultant or in

Joy of driving.
Clark scored 15 class victories or outright wins in Ford Lotus Cortina
between 1963 and 1966, including 3 hours Sebring 1965, and
2nd in class at 12 hours Sebring, 1964.

Master strokes.
Graham Turner brilliantly captures Clark likeness in 1993 portrait,
with Lotus Ford 49 and Ford-powered Indianapolis winner.

public relations. Hayes remained amazingly loyal. He persuaded Jackie Stewart to retire on the eve of his hundredth grand prix, because he said motor racing needed a live world champion. Stewart was engaged on a long-term contract with Ford.

Scott Watson stepped on Clark's toes. The individual who criticised his driving at Pau stepped on his toes. There were always things Clark would not tolerate and he used to read everything that was published about him, complaining bitterly that: "Nine times out of ten there's a mistake".

By 1970, Clark and Rindt, Chapman's two great drivers were dead. Lotus went public in 1968, with turnover up, profits doubled, and by 1969 the shares were worth twice their offer price. But even as *The Guardian* was making Chapman Young Businessman of the Year, Lotus profits were collapsing to half the level of 1968, the firm's debts were mounting, dividends dropped and the share price slumped by 90%.

To the City, it looked like a classic case of a small firm that had over-reached itself. Some rubbed their hands, for Chapman was never without his critics, customers amongst them, who found spares expensive, and despite his good press, service negligent. The least Lotus had to lose, it seemed was its independence.

Chapman remained in command until his death in 1983, fighting off crisis after crisis. He died at the height of a scandal that left questions about his financial probity unanswered. Lotus survived fuel shortages, financial stringency, plunging stock markets, and tumbling pounds; it diversified briefly into boats before being bought by other interests and continuing its crisis-laden ways.

Chapman's fall from grace coincided with that of John Zachary DeLorean who turned up in Belfast in 1978 boasting that he had $500m to build a sports car that would be safe, economical and rust-proof. Roy Mason, then Northern Ireland secretary, gave him £54 million, to set up a factory and DeLorean, who never spent another night in Belfast, built it at Dunmurry where unemployment was the highest in Europe.

DeLorean's company received subsidies of £84 million, but the factory closed in October 1982, on the day DeLorean was arrested in Los Angeles on drug charges. The world watched a video of DeLorean being arrested by men he believed were drug dealers. They were really federal agents and he poked a suitcase full of cocaine remarking: "It's better than gold," toasted the deal in champagne, then the handcuffs went on.

He was found not guilty of conspiracy to possess and distribute $24m worth of cocaine. In Detroit he was also acquitted of fraud.

In 1992 Ivan Fallon wrote a book about the debacle of DeLorean, with documents showing how $17.65m was purloined from the government money and shared out to DeLorean, Chapman, and Fred Bushell, the Lotus accountant. De Lorean claimed the money had gone to Lotus to pay for the design and construction of the prototype. Colin Chapman said he never received it, and the documents suggested both were right. They had split it 50/50, and none of it went near either company.

The court heard how DeLorean, Chapman, and Bushell siphoned off millions of pounds intended for DeLorean's company, which drew up a contract in 1978 for Lotus to develop the backbone-framed stainless-steel bodied car. Lotus needed to turn something of a sow's ear into a silk purse, for the conception of a gull-wing-doored roadster selling in large numbers was ill-conceived. The cost of the work was to be $17.65 million.

The cash was laundered in a Panamanian-registered, Geneva-based company set up by Chapman and Bushell, GPD Services Inc. None of it got anywhere near the car and, in the words of the receiver Sir Kenneth Cork, "went walkabout". A House of Commons Public Accounts Committee reported in July 1984 that the money was "misappropriated".

There was a three-way payout with De Lorean taking $8.5 million, while Chapman and Bushell divided $8,390,000 between them in numbered Swiss bank accounts. Chapman took 90 per cent, Bushell 10 per cent, or £456,000 ($848,000) including accrued interest. The bulk of the missing £9.5 million was never recovered.

The development work was carried out, but paid for directly by DeLorean, and the car went into production in 1981. Within a year the whole project was in ruins, and there was concern at the Treasury over the advances of taxpayers' money, and warnings about offshore payments from DeLorean to GPD. It took eight years for a settlement to be reached.

Fallon asserted that Chapman did not devise the wheeze on his own, but he was something of a hero to Bushell who devised offshore accounts and other money-saving schemes for him. Although Bushell's signature was on the documents, he denied having signed them. Were they forgeries? Bushel would not go as far as that, but insisted he never signed them.

Bushell was jailed for three years and fined £2.25m. Lord Justice Murray told Belfast Crown Court that he was the brains behind a "bare-faced, outrageous and massive fraud" entered into with John DeLorean and Colin Chapman. The judge said that had DeLorean not been American and beyond the court's jurisdiction, and Chapman alive, each would have been given ten-year prison terms.

DeLorean produced 8,333 cars, only 3,347 of which were sold when the factory closed. The remainder languished in distribution centres around America, or the Harland & Wolff shipyard in Belfast. An agreement was reached with DeLorean and he paid $7m on top of $9.4m already refunded to creditors. After payments from Lotus and Colin Chapman's estate, the amount recovered by the receivers reached £20m.

The best that could be said of Chapman's role in the scandal was that he chose his associates carelessly. Yet this was the man whom Jim Clark had trusted with his life.

Jim was killed four days after Jackie Stewart and John Whitmore emigrated to Switzerland. They had agreed that they would not come back in 1968 or 1969 and that Stewart would miss the British Grand Prix of 1968.

They were allowed special entry to Britain for the funeral.

The appeal to the Inland Revenue produced a further long-term result. It would no longer be necessary for tax exiles to be totally absent from the UK for 365 days on the first year of departure. Stewart was able to drive in the 1968 British Grand Prix.

The Jim Clark Foundation was set up in 1968 as an international charitable trust, with the aim of promoting and assisting research into motoring safety, both on the road and in motor racing. Research projects were financed to examine fireproof clothing for drivers, and aerodynamic devices on racing cars. Other projects were undertaken at two British universities on passenger car safety. The Foundation was based in Britain,

Last Grand Prix.
Jackie Stewart (Matra-Ford) led on lap 1, passed here by Clark (Lotus-Ford). Rindt (Brabham) third, Brabham (Brabham) and Surtees (Honda) fourth and fifth. Clark won.

Incomparable All American Racer Dan Gurney pays tribute to his friend.

but its 27 founder patrons came from seven European countries, and the United States. They included Colin Chapman, Baron Huschke von Hanstein, and Sir Alec Douglas Home, the former prime minister, who came from the Border country close to Jim Clark's home. Among other founder patrons were Count Giovanni Lurani, Peter Sellars, and Louis Chiron.

Jim Clark might have excelled in any number of ways. Had he been born in the 1920s instead of the 1930s he could have been at the controls of a fighter aircraft by 1940, not a racing car. He would have shown the same dash and brilliance, his gyros spinning, dark eyes flashing down a gunsight. He would have been cool, relaxed, professional, dedicated, and an ace. He was a protagonist who could crush opposition at will, yet would do it with such magnanimity that he would have earned the respect and devotion of adversaries and admirers alike.

Yet he would have remained an enigma. It is difficult to get a consensus view of what was at the back of his mind. He loved motor racing. It was not like work; it was fun although when it became serious for him one wonders if it really was so much fun at the end.

Walter Hayes reminded me at the dinner in Edinburgh to mark the 25th anniversary of Jim's death, a clan gathering he called it since it was both a family and a Scottish occasion, of another of Dr Johnson's observations. Sam Johnson discovered many things on his tour of Scotand in 1773 and believed it was the clan feeling that enabled Scots to achieve for themselves in England, "…a success which rather exceeded the due proportion of their real merit."

Johnson put this down to the fact that while the Irish were a fair people, – "They never speak well of one another." The Scots had "A disposition to tell lies in favour of each other".

There was no need for me to try to tell anything less than the truth, as I saw it, about Jim Clark in this book. I spoke to the matchless Dan Gurney about him at Ketteringham Hall, formerly Team Lotus's design headquarters when they were launching Andrew Ferguson's book on Lotus's years at Indianapolis.

Tall, spare, thoughtful, Dan signed the picture of them both at the Speedway. "You know Eric," he said with a sigh. "He was a very special guy." Clever man. He summed Jim up in half a dozen words better than I have in all 70,000.

"These Scots," said Hayes, "Who lie lovingly about each other's achievements always get it right when the time for summing-up arrives."

So did Dan Gurney. Jim Clark was indeed very special.

ACKNOWLEDGEMENTS AND BIBLIOGRAPHY

The author and publisher Ruth Dymock thank Ford Motor Company, in particular John Southgate, vice president of public and governmental affairs for their enthusiastic backing for a new book on Jim Clark. It also enjoyed the support of John's distinguished predecessor Walter Hayes who was closely involved with Jim Clark's career. Practical assistance came from throughout the Ford family including the director of public and governmental affairs Michael Callaghan, and Ford's corporate affairs staff Don Hume, Simon Sproule, Maggie Sweeting, Isabella Nash, and Stuart Dyble. Thanks are due to Barry Reynolds, his staff at Ford Photographic for searching the archives for Jim Clark pictures and David Burgess-Wise.

Thanks also go to individuals who gave time, talked, and reminisced including David Benson, Bill Cormie, Jabby Crombac, Dan Gurney, Walter Hayes, Peter Hetherington, Patrick Mennem, Stirling Moss, Geoff Murdoch, Bill Potts, Andrew Russell, Jackie Stewart, Ed and Sally Swart, Rob Walker, and Ian Scott Watson. We were especially pleased to have the co-operation of Jim's family, Douglas and Isobel Henderson, Don and Betty Peddie, Alec and Mattie Calder, and Ken Smith.

A testimony to the affection and admiration in which Jim Clark was held throughout motor racing was that so many individuals offered contributions – more than it proved possible to accommodate. To them also the author offers his sincere thanks.

We are indebted to the work of previous authors on Jim Clark. We have drawn on material by Bill Gavin, Doug Nye, and in particular Graham Gauld who gave us his generous support. The late Andrew Ferguson's splendid book on Lotus at Indianapolis appeared just in time to add extra information to this important period. Photographers and other researchers whose help was invaluable include Michael Cooper, David Phipps, and Nigel Snowdon, veterans and contemporaries of the years spent together covering Jim Clark's grand prix career. We were pleased to include Bill Henderson's work; not only his early Scottish photographs but also his paintings of Loretto and the 1955 Scottish Rally. There are photographs by Benno Müller, Bernard Cahier, Julius Weitmann, Franco Lini, Patrick Benjafield, Yves Debraine and Ewen Forsyth.

No book on Jim Clark would be complete without the art of Michael Turner, another close contemporary of the 1960s, and Graham Turner's uncannily perceptive portrait. Dexter Brown's poignant portrait on the jacket was painted in 1968. Alan Fearnley's oil sketch of the victory at Zandvoort is reproduced by courtesy of David and Chris Mills of Grand Prix Sportique. This painting and the race programmes shown are in the author's collection. The 1965 cartoon series by Boivent Duffar, text by Jabby Crombac, are reproduced by kind permission of the copyright holders.

Our thanks are also due to H C Alldridge O.L. MA and Keith Budge MA Cert Ed of Loretto, David Bann, Pierre Bardinon, John Blunsden, Neil Brown, Barry Bolton, Harry Calton, Hazel Chapman, Clive Chapman, Peter Gethin, Ivan Fallon, Max le Grand, Alan Henry, Innes Ireland, Diane Lappage, Eric Liddell, Anthony Marsh, Brian Melia, Doug Niven, Nigel Roebuck, David Ross, Paul Ross, Cedric Selzer, Dick Scammell, Jimmy Stewart, Eoin Young, Tom Walkinshaw, and the Borders Museum Service which is responsible for the Jim Clark Room at Duns.

Bibliography

Jim Clark at the Wheel, Arthur Barker, London 1964

The Jim Clark Story, by Bill Gavin, Leslie Frewin, London 1968

Jim Clark, Portrait of a great driver, by Graham Gauld, Hamlyn, Feltham Middlesex 1968

Jim Clark by Doug Nye, Hazleton, Richmond, Surrey 1991.

The Grand Prix Greats, Barrie Gill, Pelham, London 1972.

Jim Clark Remembered, by Graham Gauld, Patrick Stephens Wellingborough 1975.

Colin Chapman, The Man and his Cars, by Gerard Crombac, Patrick Stephens, Wellingborough 1986.

Jim Clark, The Legend Lives On, by Graham Gauld, Patrick Stephens, Sparkford, Somerset 1989.

The Complete History of Grand Prix Motor Racing, by Adriano Cimarosti, Motor Racing Publications, Croydon, Surrey 1990.

Ecurie Ecosse, by Graham Gauld, Graham Gauld PR, Edinburgh 1992.

Archie and the Listers, by Robert Edwards, Patrick Stephens, Sparkford, Somerset 1995.

Grand Prix Data Book, by David Hayhoe and David Holland, David Hayhoe, Croydon, Surrey 1995.

Lotus, The Indianapolis Years, by Andrew Ferguson and Doug Nye, Patrick Stephens, Sparkford, Somerset 1996.

The Grand Prix Who's Who, by Steve Small, Guinness Publishing, Enfield, Middlesex 1996.

Among the magazines used in research were *The Motor, The Autocar, Autosport, Motor World, Top Gear, the magazine of the Scottish Sporting Car Club*, and *Motor Sport*, to whose proprietors motoring historians owe continuing thanks.

INDEX